RIDING AND SCHOOLING HORSES

Plate I *Lt. Col. Chamberlin on "Pleasant Smile" during three-day equestrian championship. Members of winning team.*

RIDING AND SCHOOLING HORSES

By HARRY D. CHAMBERLIN

Lieutenant-Colonel of Cavalry,
United States Army

INTRODUCTION TO THE ORIGINAL EDITION BY

HONORABLE JOHN CUDAHY

INTRODUCTION TO THE XENOPHON PRESS EDITION BY

WARREN MATHA

Available at www.XenophonPress.com
Copyright © 1934 by Mrs. Helen B. Chamberlin
Copyright © 2020 by Xenophon Press LLC

Illustrated by Paul Brown

All rights reserved. No part of this work may be reproduced or transmitted in any form or by any means, electronic or mechanical, including photocopying, or by any information storage or retrieval system except by written permission from the publisher.

Published by Xenophon Press LLC
Nassawadox, Virginia 23413, U.S.A.
xenophonpress@gmail.com

Hardcover ISBN: 978-1948717199
Epub ISBN: 978-1948717205

INTRODUCTION TO THE XENOPHON PRESS EDITION

One sentence captures the origins of Brigadier General Harry Dwight Chamberlin's contributions to horsemanship: "Genius finds invisible links between things."

Chamberlin's genius links a modified concept of Italian forward riding with French dressage and the American cavalry's vast experience in riding long distances. His enduring legacy provides not only the foundation for what George Morris calls the "American jumping style" but also for so much more. The totality of Chamberlin's writing provides a complete protocol to train both horse and rider for Eventing, Show Jumping, Endurance Riding, Hunting, and just plain hacking for fun.

Chamberlin's writings remain a trove of wisdom wrought from years of experience and of theory learned from years of study. As Captain Paul Kendal, one of the best instructors in the Horsemanship Detachment at Ft. Riley, advises: "if you read only one book on riding, then it should be *Riding and Schooling Horses*."

In the twentifirst Century: The Olympic champion William Steinkraus writes in 2008, "So often, I think I have come up with an idea of my own, only to find it in one of Chamberlin's books." James Wofford contends that Chamberlin remains second only to Caprilli in international influence and that "Chamberlin is to horsemanship as Mozart is to music." Charles Chenevix-Trench writes that Chamberlin "…had an influence on American riding second to none…" George Morris ranks Chamberlin as "the 20th Century's greatest combined horseman, theorist, teacher, and writer."

Chamberlin's writings offer a treasure trove of practical knowledge. As the 20th century's preeminent American cavalryman, he offers principles to train eventers and jumpers to compete at the Olympic level and endurance horses to ride 30 miles a day indefinitely over all types of terrain or to ride between 100 and 170 miles in 24 hours. Chamberlin believes that all such effort rests on a common foundation: dressage inspired by the French at Saumur.

Today, no one equals Chamberlin's education and training; no one equals his range of experience and accomplishment. When you consider his career…a distinguished graduate of three great schools of advanced horsemanship, a cavalry General, horseman, teacher, trainer, three-time-Olympian, author, and equestrian theorist… you consider a genius not only in the development of theory but in its application as well.

In *Riding and Schooling Horses*, Chamberlin states his essential principles of horsemanship. Just a few of the insights one finds in its pages:

The seat: The upper body always must incline at least a trifle to the front; ever so slightly with long stirrups; progressively more forward the shorter the stirrups. Except for variations in the length of the stirrups and the forward inclination of the upper body, the seat remains the same throughout all aspects of riding.

The secure seat: No matter how experienced the rider, **ride** without stirrups as often as possible.

The posting trot: let *the thrust of the horse* push you forward and slightly upward out of the saddle and then let yourself come back down lightly and sparingly. Note again: the thrust of the horse pushes the rider out of the saddle. The rider's leg muscles do *not* lift the rider up and forward. This concept proves extremely important in long distance riding to conserve the rider's strength.

The horse's personality: the horse remembers everything. "His memory…is infallible." *"Reward should instantly follow obedience; and punishment, disobedience"*

The hands: Chamberlin discusses the "hands" at length and refers to the writings of James Fillis on this issue. The reader will find in Volume Two the James Fillis discussion of "the hands." Chamberlin repeatedly warns against "over flexion" especially direct flexion. Chamberlin adopts the concept of the "fixed hand" in that the rider should fix the position of the hand with reins stretched, arms and elbows set; then the fingers tighten intermittently if necessary. Once the horse "gives" the fingers immediately give, the hands and arms relax and also give. He discusses the concept of "vibrations" on the rein.

The legs: Chamberlin writes that the legs should ask for impulsion but only when necessary to maintain or to change the gait. Chamberlin writes the "calves of rider's legs *squeeze when necessary* to make horse walk fast and freely." (*Italics added*) This recommendation to "squeeze when necessary" comports with the French concept of squeezing the legs only when the rider requires a change in gait or when the horse slows the gait without the rider's asking for same.

Chamberlin discusses, at length, the French theories regarding the coordination of hands with leg for changes in direction and reproduces the diagrams depicting this coordination originated at the School of Versailles and introduced at Saumur by General Benoist.

The Issue of Collection: Chamberlin writes that the French school of training produces a "more clever and pleasant horse to ride *if it is done* *properly.*" He writes: "In general, these horses are over-bitted and poorly ridden. As a result, the necks are too much arched and over flexed…It is undoubtedly true that except when executed by expert riders, too much collection and schooling are apt to ruin a horse entirely, than are too little."

Regarding collection itself, Chamberlin warns: "For the most part, a high state of collection is totally unnecessary, and except with the most finished riders, is the proverbial 'razor in the hands of a monkey.' The almost invariable result of demanding high collection is over-flexion. The horse finally develops a permanently over-arched neck; his gaits become high and short; he loses the faculty of extending his neck and going calmly…*The moral indicated is that direct flexion should be very carefully and sparingly employed.*"

He repeatedly cautions against "over-flexion." Recall that the French master de la Guérinière advises against collection for the outdoor horse in his writings as well. While Chamberlin opposes heavy handed collection, he suggests a more "natural" collection that the horse would develop on its own or through exercises such as riding down hills to bring the horse's rear legs underneath the horse. In this respect, he seems more Italian than French.

Jumping: Chamberlin breaks jumping down into four phases: the approach, the take-off, the period of suspension, the landing. One should read these sections repeatedly.

Chamberlin starts riding in childhood but studies in depth all things equine at West Point. He then graduates first in his class from the basic and advanced horsemanship courses at Ft. Riley. Later, as the U.S. Army's official observer, he analyzes the horsemanship of the French at Saumur, the Germans at Hannover, the Belgians at Ypres, and the British at Weedon. French lightness and German precision appeal to him. Later still, as a distinguished graduate of Saumur, he understands and applies French dressage expertly. As a distinguished graduate of Tor di Quinto, he masters Italian forward riding; on graduation day, the school's Commandant presents a diploma to Chamberlin and says: "the pupil has surpassed his master."

Over time, Chamberlin develops theories of horsemanship: his "Chamberlin seat" modifies the Italian forward seat to render the rider more secure and more precise with the aides. He applies French dressage to train jumpers and cavalry mounts… something the Italian theorists and many others refuse to do. Ultimately, Chamberlin combines and then transcends the equestrian theories of France, Germany, Italy, and the United States to create a mode of riding and training that elevates the U.S. Cavalry's horsemanship to its highest plain and that influences Olympic riders throughout the world to this day.

To forward his theories, Chamberlin writes *Riding and Schooling Horses*, then *Training Hunters, Jumpers, and Hacks*. He supervises the 1942 revision of the U.S. Cavalry's bible *Horsemanship and Horsemastership*. He refines the training methods of the Army's Cavalry Replacement Training Center at Fort Riley. One observes similar methods today at the French National Riding School at Saumur and the German National Riding School at Warendorf.

Regarding Chamberlin's range of experience, space allows only an abridged summary. In 1912, he rides in the Philippines where heat prostration causes cavalrymen to fall from their saddles but his unit never loses a horse. In 1916, he rides with the 5th Cavalry over 1,000 miles round-trip through Mexico under war-time conditions, over the most difficult terrain on earth, where temperatures soar to 120 degrees by day and canteens freeze solid at night. Throughout the late 1920s on Tanbark, he defeats the finest horseman of Germany, Ireland, Poland, Holland, France and Britain in successive international show jumping competitions. In 1926, he captains and trains the 8th Cavalry polo team. It wins the national polo championship (an Army first) and he achieves a 3-goal (professional) handicap.

In 1932, at the Olympics, he and the riders he trains win the Team Gold Medal for Eventing riding in the Chamberlin style on horses trained in the Chamberlin fashion. In Eventing, Chamberlin achieves the best dressage score of all competitors. Later, on the morning of the *Prix des Nations* competition, his jumper Tanbark turns up lame. So, Chamberlin rides a mare on which he has not competed before and wins the Silver Individual Medal as 105,000 spectators look on. Chamberlin's jumping style proves so spectacular that Vladimir Littauer tells his students: "… don't bother to try to go over obstacles the way Major Chamberlin does, because you will never be able to do it anyway …"

On the last day of the Olympics of 1932, Chamberlin's military career requires that he retire from international competition. He is 45. His superiors recognize him as one of the most competent, respected, and well-liked officers of his generation. They slate him for the army's highest commands. Just as he achieves his first overseas mission early in World War II, terminal cancer begins to ravage his athletic frame. He passed away in 1944 at age 57.

In a life cut short, Chamberlin provides several lifetimes of insight. He writes: "Nothing, aside from the dearest human relationships, can give the pleasure found in working and playing with a horse." So, read on…and then go and do likewise.

Warren Matha
February 2020

FOREWORD

General Chamberlin's vast knowledge and experience in riding and schooling horses makes the title of this book a "natural." The popularity of the previous editions of "Riding and Schooling Horses" has proven that it has been accepted as the best American book on the subject.

Certainly no person was more qualified to write a book on this subject as he was one of the outstanding American horsemen and instructors in horsemastership during his lifetime.

His successful participation in many of the Olympic Equestrian Games and other foreign shows against the world's top riders established for him an international reputation as an expert horseman.

Although "Riding and Schooling Horses" was written primarily for the novice, it also can be read and studied advantageously by the more experienced horseman.

This limited edition of "Riding and Schooling Horses" is published by the Armored Cavalry Journal for the purpose of furthering a better understanding and knowledge of horsemastership to the ever growing fraternity of Equestrians.

> EDWIN M. SUMNER
> Colonel, Cavalry,
> Editor *Armored Cavalry Journal*
> Washington, D. C.
> June, 1947

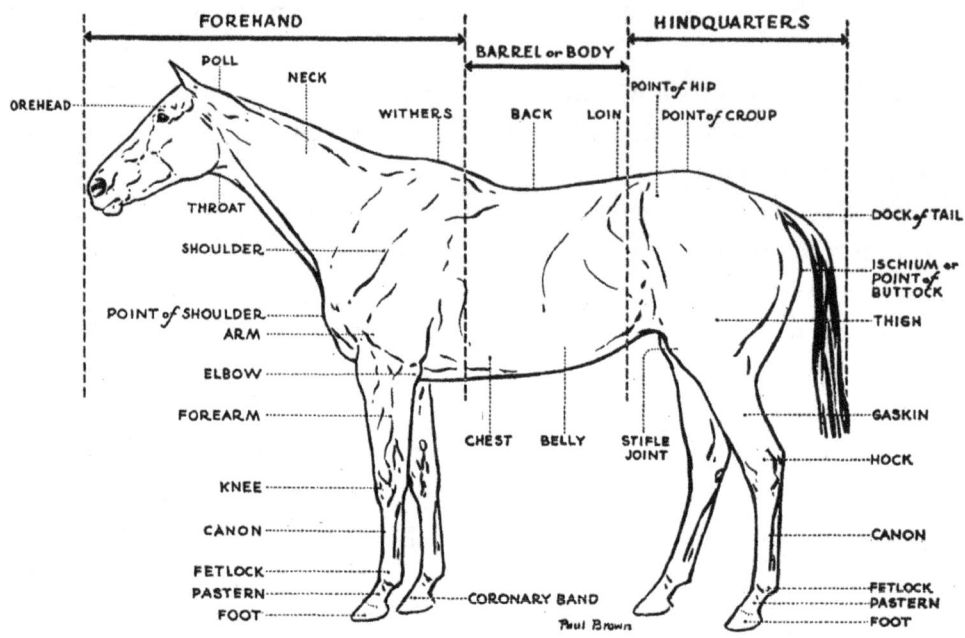

Plate II *Exterior of the Horse*

PREFACE

The correct principles of equitation and horse training are in themselves simple and well-defined, and easily within the comprehension of any intelligent mind. Unfortunately, these principles are so difficult to find in the mass of literature on equestrian subjects, and often so intermingled with inaccurate and abstruse statements, that the most earnest student in his search for them is frequently discouraged.

Moreover, the precepts set forth by some of the most able authors of former times, are so tersely expressed, and presuppose so much equestrian knowledge, that their full meaning and importance are difficult to grasp unless the reader has had much practical experience. Oftentimes instructors, through limited knowledge or inability to make their instruction understood, teach their students little. Though the instructors are painstaking, and the written word is available, students, despite their zeal, finish their courses with many misconceptions, and only a vague knowledge concerning the horse and riding.

Equitation is not mysterious, either in theory or in practice. A good horseman requires a normally alert mind, with an analytical turn, which always asks "why" and "how" about the horse and his training. He needs only an average physique, which can soon be coordinated by his alert mind and regular practice at riding. No great strength or other remarkable physical attributes are necessary.

In addition, he should possess a theoretical knowledge of training and the use of the aids, along with a correct conception of the seat, and how to ride it. The purpose of this book is to present clearly the fundamental principles of equitation and horse training, with rules and examples which explain and illustrate the seat, and the use of the hands and legs as aids. Every effort has been made to eliminate the unessential, and to include and emphasize the indispensable.

After describing, in Chapter I, the Forward Seat, (a name erroneously applied in the United States to innumerable grotesque postures), Chapter II is devoted to an explanation of how the seat is maintained when the horse is in motion. After all, it is a simple matter to place anyone in the correct position on a stationary horse, but to hold that seat under the reactions resulting from a fast gallop, he must have some preliminary theoretical knowledge of what to do, and what sensations are felt, when riding correctly.

Chapter III deals with the Horse's Personality. Therein are found the principles deduced from equine psychology, on which riding and training must be based. These principles are also readily understood, but in practice, a horseman must continually analyze the actions of his hands and legs when used as aids, in order to determine whether or not those actions are in accord with the principles. Otherwise, there is no progress in training.

In Chapter IV, The Aids, the subject of "Hands" is the most elusive to express. However, a sincere effort has been made to furnish a few general rules which dictate the use of the hands under any difficult circumstances which may arise, as well as certain explicit rules with concrete examples of their application.

Space does not permit embracing the particular routine followed in the breaking and training of colts destined to become hunters, polo ponies, jumpers, or hacks. However, Chapter VI, Marks of a Trained Mount, briefly sketches the objectives and the sequence of training necessary to produce a well-mannered mount for any purpose. All require this same basic training.

Jumping, which enters as an unusual incident in riding, is discussed separately in Chapter VII, since, being a special gymnastic for horse and rider, it is best treated individually.

It may be of interest for the reader to know that every page of the manuscript was submitted to an inexperienced horsewoman, in order to ascertain whether she could understand every point in the book, and could put each step into practice. In any case where she was unable to follow the book in theory or in practice, that part was rewritten until it was entirely clear.

Throughout, repetitions of salient facts have been purposely made. These facts are those which have been frequently misunderstood, or, in many cases, not understood at all. Indulgence is begged if too much emphasis seems laid on certain topics. They are basic, and those which will always require most study and attention from all riders, regardless of experience.

Apology is offered for frequent digressions in the chapters and under sub-titles. This, too, was done purposely in the desire to bring out the close interrelation of the various subjects which were discussed individually for the sake of clarity in presentation.

It is urged that the reader constantly refer to the instructions relative to that particular phase of riding or training in which he is engaged. It was only after many years of intensive riding that the writer fully appreciated the significance of the sententious maxims read in the works of the old masters. As the rider's "feel" of the horse develops, old sayings take on new meanings.

For the Seat advocated, the writer is principally indebted to the Italian Cavalry School at Tor di Quinto. The Italians were the pioneers in riding the forward seat during cross-country work and jumping. However, the teachings of the French and American Cavalry Schools, modified to some extent by observation of the best horsemen among the Germans, Swedes, and Poles, have entered into the conception of the Seat described. Much personal experience has convinced the writer of its practical superiority.

Since Xenophon, who wrote well on the subject, there have been, through all the centuries, some men who rode and wrote; some, who rode and wrote not; some, who wrote and rode not. It is unfortunate that so little of the best has been translated into English.

La Guérinière, Baucher, Le Comte D'Aure, and many other brilliant French horsemen have handed down in writing the precepts derived from their own great skill and that of their predecessors. These teachings, but little altered, and used for generations at the French Cavalry School at Saumur, have been adopted almost in toto by the American Cavalry School at Fort Riley, Kansas. There is nothing better in the world concerning the training and schooling of the horse. The instruction received at Saumur and Fort Riley, and found in the works of the great masters, provides the basis for all that pertains to the Aids and Training in this book.

All the authors to whom the writer is deeply indebted could not be thanked. His gratitude is also due to horsemen of many nations from whom instruction, advice, and ideas have been gleaned, both in school and in competition. Last but not least, to those numberless, noble horses with which he has associated through so many happy hours, heartfelt thanks are owed. Along with sport and pleasure, they have provided the experience, practice, and crystallized knowledge which no books can give.

Harry Dwight Chamberlin

To

HELEN BRADMAN CHAMBERLIN

CONTENTS

Introduction to the Xenophon Press Edition by Warren Matha i

Foreword by Edwin M. Sumner v

Preface vii

Introduction xv

I. The Seat 1

II. How to Learn and Ride the Forward Seat 25

III. The Horse's Personality 47

IV. The Aids 55

V. Bits 103

VI. Marks of a Trained Mount 107

VII. Jumping 115

Xenophon Press Library 133

List of Photographs

I. LT. COL. CHAMBERLIN ON "PLEASANT SMILE" .... Frontispiece

II. EXTERIOR OF THE HORSE vi

III. SAUMUR SEAT 3

IV. FRENCH OFFICER 3

V. ITALIAN OFFICER 5

VI. SWEDISH OFFICER 5

VII. GERMAN OFFICER 5

VIII. STIRRUPS CORRECT LENGTH FOR JUMPING 7

IX. STIRRUPS CORRECTLY ADJUSTED FOR HACKING OR HUNTING FORWARD INCLINATION OF BODY 7

X. SAUMUR TYPE OF SADDLE 13

XI. ITALIAN SADDLE 13

XII. POLISH SADDLE 13

XIII. POORLY-CONSTRUCTED SADDLE 13

XIV. CORRECT POSITION WHEN USING SHORT STIRRUPS 15

XV. STANDING IN STIRRUPS 20

XVI. SEATED AFTER STANDING IN STIRRUPS 20

XVII. INCORRECT SEAT 23

XVIII. CORRECT SEAT WITH NORMAL LENGTH OF STIRRUP-STRAPS 23

XIX. SEAT WITHOUT STIRRUPS 30

XX. TEACHING HORSE LONG, FREE, STRIDING WALK 35

XXI. POSTING ON RIGHT DIAGONAL 37

XXII. POSTING ON RIGHT DIAGONAL 37

XXIII. SEATED IN SADDLE AT GALLOP 40

XXIV. SEATED FULLY AT GALLOP 42

XXV. LAST BEAT OF GALLOP STRIDE	43
XXVI. RIDING IN STIRRUPS	45
XXVII. RIDING IN STIRRUPS	45
XXVIII.	46
XXIX. "BUDDIES"	51
XXX. HANDS FOLLOWING HORSE'S HEAD	54
XXXI. HOLDING SINGLE REIN	54
XXXII. NORMAL POSITION OF HANDS	56
XXXIII. REINS A TRIFLE TOO LONG	58
XXXIV. REINS CORRECTLY ADJUSTED IN LENGTH	58
XXXV. HANDS "FIXED"	65
XXXVI. PRODUCING "VIBRATIONS"	69
XXXVII. RIGHT WRIST BENDS INWARD AND UPWARD	69
XXXVIII. HIGHLY-COLLECTED HIGH SCHOOL HORSE	75
XXXIX. HANDS EXECUTING "HALF-HALT"	77
XL. HORSE "STAR-GAZING"	81
XLI. MILD DOUBLE BRIDLE	83
XLII. WELL-TRAINED HORSES	102
XLIII. TEACHING HORSE TO EXTEND TROT	109
XLIV. "TANBARK"	114
XLV. FEET NOT HOME IN STIRRUPS	121
XLVI. DOWNWARD THRUST OF HEAD AND NECK	121
XLVII. ENGAGEMENT OF HOCKS	123
XLVIII. FORELEGS HAVING CLEARED, RIDER REMAINS OUT OF SADDLE	123
XLIX. RESULT OF LOSING SEAT DURING APPROACH	125
L. BEAUTIFUL FORM	125
LI. BEAUTIFUL BALANCE	127
LII. FRACTION OF SECOND BEFORE LANDING	130
LIII. ONE FORELEG GROUNDED	130
LIV. RIDER'S LEGS SLIPPED TO REAR	131
LV. LOWER LEGS IN CORRECT POSITION	131

List of Diagrams

A. Sketches showing forward inclination of body necessary to ride in balance.. 10

B. Sketches showing rein effects
Sketch 1. FIRST REIN EFFECT 87
Sketch 2. SECOND REIN EFFECT 89
Sketch 3. THIRD REIN EFFECT 91
Sketch 4. FOURTH REIN EFFECT 93
Sketch 5. FIFTH REIN EFFECT 95

INTRODUCTION

Here, at last, is the book we have been hopefully awaiting for years; a plain spoken, factual explanation of the principles underlying horsemanship, which for some reason all writers since Baucher's time have obscured in a mist of baffling, undefined technicalities.

Many of us suspected that this lack of clarity was the deliberate affectation of equestrian pedantry, yet we had no remedy.

Now comes Colonel Chamberlin and in direct, simple language presents an account of riding and training horses for the show ring and for hunting which the rawest novice can understand and which the most experienced horseman will ponder. His discussion of The Seat, Hands, Jumping, Application of the Aids, and Fundamental Riding Precepts, should be read and reread many times. The Chamberlin seat, an eclectic evolution of broad experience, is set forth with unanswerable common sense and logic.

Few men in the horse world have had the advantage of the author's education: a graduate of Tor di Quinto, Italy, and Saumur, France, and of the United States Cavalry School at Fort Riley; observer at the German school at Hanover, and at Weedon, England; instructor at Fort Riley and West Point; member of the American team at the Inter-Allied games in Paris, 1919; member of famous teams at the 1920 and 1928 Olympics, and captain of the victorious one at Los Angeles in 1932. Leader of the successful United States teams in international military competitions: 1929, 1930, 1931, he has with his team mates also participated in horse shows held in Poland, Ireland, France and Germany and has assimilated, not only the wisdom of the past, but the practice of the present.

Impressive as this great range of training and experience is, it cannot account for a Chamberlin, for a truly great horseman is a genius, endowed with the fine sensibilities of an artist, combined with keen perception, cool judgment, courage, discretion, unfailing patience and infinite tact.

John Cudahy
Embassy of the United States of America
August 11, 1934

CHAPTER I

THE SEAT

Form in Riding

Only in the last thirty years, after centuries of riding, has the mechanically correct, forward seat been developed. The ever-increasing interest in equestrian sports, such as polo, flat racing, steeplechasing, and show jumping has gradually caused progressive horsemen to search for a seat which would be most advantageous mechanically to the horse, and which would therefore permit him to beat his more poorly ridden rivals. This is just another way of saying that an attempt to develop better "form" in riding has been constantly in progress. The almost-daily shattering of world's records in swimming, running, pole-vaulting, golf, and all other branches of athletics presents a convincing testimonial to the increased efficiency produced by perfecting form. Where there is no competition, there is generally little incentive toward improvement in form, except perhaps in manual labor, where laziness acts as a spur in devising short cuts. Since fox hunting is pleasure, not labor, and since competition is largely lacking in that otherwise glorious sport, an excuse for the lack of form and efficiency in what is usually called "the hunting seat" presents itself. How such an ungraceful manner of riding, so punishing to a horse, could have persisted among horsemen for so long, is amazing.

That great American jockey, "Tod" Sloan, was the first man to support his weight on his knees and in the stirrups, and lean his body forward over the horse's shoulders, when riding flat races. The story has been told that an impetuous horse jerked Sloan forward out of the saddle, and ran away with both him and the race. Sloan's keen mind detected something advantageous in this forward position, — involuntarily assumed in the first instance, — and promptly evolved his racing seat. His astounding success in England and at home soon resulted in all jockeys copying his style of seat in flat racing. Incidentally, this forward racing seat is known abroad as "the American seat."

Shortly after Sloan's victories, Captain Federico Caprilli, an Italian Army officer, modified this racing seat somewhat, and introduced the Italian one for cross-country riding and jumping. Caprilli's seat, when finally officially adopted, gained many successes for all Italian officers' riding teams, which participated in the great International Shows at Nice, Rome, Berlin, Olympia in London, and elsewhere. There was no doubt as to its superiority, since it gave the horse more freedom in using his entire ability when negotiating large obstacles, or racing across broken country. Soon all discerning horsemen of other nations began imitating, to some extent, the Italian seat. The Italian Cavalry Schools at Pinerolo and Tor di Quinto developed a number of high-class riders, and many nations, including our own, sent Cavalry officers to these two schools, through the courtesy of the Italian government.

Italian, French, and Other Systems Compared

Briefly, the Italian teachings are to the effect that; first, the horse should be allowed great liberty in the use of his head and neck, and no effort should be exerted, through training, to make him shift more of his weight to the hind quarters[1] than he naturally carries on them; second, the rider's weight should be kept well forward over the horse's shoulders, through inclining the body to the front.

The Italians, therefore, go to an extreme, in that their horses receive little training to develop suppleness of poll and jaw, or to raise the head and neck in order to make them lightly-balanced.[2] As they carry much of their own and the rider's weight on their forehands,[3] it would be necessary to completely re-train them for use as polo ponies, or to bring out any of the brilliance and handiness which is developed by suppling the poll and jaw, and raising the head and neck. The latter training shifts a larger proportion of the horse's weight to the hind quarters when at the slow gaits, turning quickly, or slowing down and halting. It produces a more clever and pleasant horse to ride; if it is properly done.

For more than a hundred years, the French School for Cavalry officers at Saumur has been world-famous. Its seat has not gone to the extremes in forward inclination of the body and shortness of stirrup-straps that are found in that of the Italian School. French horses receive far more schooling

---

[1] Hind quarters. See Plate II, The Exterior of the Horse

[2] Lightly-balanced. See "lightness," page 76, Chapter IV.

[3] Forehand. See Plate II, The Exterior of the Horse.

Plate III *Saumur Seat. (1923)*

Plate IV *French officer.*

for the purpose of producing suppleness, brilliance, and handiness. When trained by good riders, they have delightful manners. In general, however, these horses, like so many of our own, in the Army and out, are over-bitted and poorly ridden. As a result, their necks are too much arched and over-flexed,[4] with the attendant evils, to be described later. It is undoubtedly true that, except when executed by expert riders, too much collection[5] and schooling are more apt to ruin a horse entirely, than are too little. As in the case of so many other things, the middle course in training seems the safest, soundest, and surest.

The Italian seat is, perhaps, for most horsemen, a little too radical, in that the stirrup-straps are always exceedingly short, and as will be shown later, the shorter the stirrup-strap, the greater must be the inclination of the body to the front, in order to ride in balance. On the other hand, the French seat, which is apparently being modified in the direction of the Italian one, especially for jumping, still resembles somewhat that of the classic haute école.[6] The Swedish and German Schools correctly believe in long and thorough schooling, but teach the horse to take a very firm support on his bit. Their seats are not generally as far forward as the Italian one, nor are they, in consequence, as conducive to comfort and freedom for the horse. For jumping and cross-country riding, the Italians undoubtedly have the correct principles regarding the seat, but as regards principles of training and schooling the horse, those of the French are equal to, if not better than any others in the world. In the United States, a great many of our foremost riders in the Cavalry are following a system of training and riding which has sought to extract the best from all the foreign schools, and have added thereto the elements of value discovered here in the United States.

In every country abroad, the military riders, as a whole, are outstanding as compared to civilians. This is only natural, since normally the officers ride habitually in their profession, and also for years have received the benefit of scientific instruction at the Cavalry schools. Certain countries, — Belgium, Poland, Holland, Rumania, and others, — have their own schools, and their little differences in type of seat, as well as system of training. However, for the most part all have followed the teachings of the French, Italians, or Germans. Credit is entirely due to Italy for the forward seat, which, with

---

[4] Over-flexed. Neck greatly rounded over, with head drawn toward the breast.

[5] Collection. See page 74, Chapter IV.

[6] Haute école. High-school training consists of certain artificial gaits or "airs," which involve much collection, springiness, and action of hocks and knees. The following are examples: Piaffer, — a cadenced trot in place; passage, — a very lofty, springy trot; changes of lead on straight lines, even to executing the changes at each stride.

Plate V *Italian officer.*

Plate VI *Swedish officer*

Plate VII *German officer*

modifications, will assuredly become universal, as its merit is indisputable as far as the basic principles upon which it is founded are concerned. There are doubtlessly certain changes which can be profitably made, notably in the length of stirrup to be used, except when jumping.

Length of Stirrup-Straps

The stirrup leathers should always be adjusted in length according to the type of riding which is done.

It is well known that to favor maximum speed, all jockeys ride with exceedingly short stirrups. This permits them to keep the weight entirely off the saddle seat by supporting it in their stirrups and on their knees, which, due to the short stirrup-straps, are thrust far forward. Thus, when a jockey rides with his body crouched over the horse's shoulders and neck, wind resistance is diminished, and the horse's back, loin, and hind quarters, which furnish the driving power, are unhindered. Also, the horse's equilibrium is more unstable toward the front, — (a condition favoring speed), — as the jockey's mass is supported almost directly over the forelegs. Since all the motive power comes from the hind legs, and since the horse, when galloping, only uses his forelegs as a pole vaulter uses his pole in vaulting, the racing seat over the shoulders is mechanically of great advantage to the race-horse. It has the disadvantages of being most uncomfortable for the rider over any long period of time, and of being insecure if the horse makes any violent or unexpected movements, particularly sideways. The shorter the stirrup-straps, the greater becomes the insecurity of the seat. Then comes the thought that since long stirrups make for security, why not always have them extremely long, as do the cowboys? The answer is that such long stirrups are only suited to certain types of saddles, as, for instance, the western cowboys', and obviously the seat resulting from such long stirrups is disadvantageous, both to horse and rider in sports like polo, hunting, steeplechasing, and jumping. For these sports, different lengths of stirrups are required in order to allow the horse to put forth his greatest efforts with maximum efficiency under the handicap of the rider's weight, as well as to allow the rider more comfort and security.

The principles of the seat advocated herein remain the same for all types of riding. There are only minor variations in the length of stirrup-straps, and in the resultant change in the forward inclination of the body. It will be found that the shorter the stirrup becomes, the more the body must be inclined to the front to remain in perfect balance, and thus minimize interference with the horse's efforts.

Plate VIII *Stirrups shorted to correct length for jumping high obstacles. Note slight forward inclination of body. (Feet not far enough in stirrups.)*

Plate IX *Stirrups correctly adjusted for hacking or hunting. Note difference in length of stirrups and inclination of rider's body between this and preceeding illustration.*

Therefore, following the rule just given, the jockey with the extremely short stirrups leans far forward over the horse's shoulders. Next, in the case of steeplechase riders, the stirrups are somewhat longer than in flat racing, since when racing over obstacles, there is obviously need for a more secure seat. Also, the body of the expert steeplechase rider is inclined well forward, although not so much as that of the flat race jockey, since the former's stirrups are not quite so short. In show jumping the stirrups should be quite short, and the body, as a result, is inclined far forward to establish balance, or, as is said, — "be with the horse." At this point, it is emphatically remarked that the forward inclination of the body is accomplished by leaning forward at the hip joints. NOT by humping the backbone, which is an unsightly, powerless position, and has nothing to do with the correct forward seat.

Stirrups for Hunting

To continue; — when hunting, where the horse must jump, gallop across rough country, and keep going sometimes for hours during a "long day," the stirrups must be sufficiently long for the rider to be secure and fairly comfortable. Naturally, on the other hand, any true sportsman wants to give his horse every advantage. Therefore the stirrups should be as short as is consistent with security and reasonable comfort, since there is no doubt that the short stirrup, with a correct seat, makes all jumping and galloping much easier for a horse. However, as is so often seen, where a rider has short stirrups, but sits bolt upright or leans to the rear, with his knees high, so that all his weight rests at one spot on the cantle[7] of the saddle, the short stirrup becomes a positive disadvantage to both horse and rider. In this grotesque position, the man's weight hammers the horse's loin at every stride and jump, causing him great fatigue as well as pain. Note the resentment a hunter, so ridden, displays as he hits the ground after a jump. His ears fly back, and often he kicks out violently or endeavors to run away, upon receiving as a regard for a gallant effort in clearing an obstacle, the thud, on his back and loin, of his thoughtless passenger's weight. So a short stirrup is disadvantageous for man and horse, unless the body is inclined forward from the hips, so as to keep the greater part of the rider's mass on the forelegs. The old theory about keeping the weight far to the rear toward the center of the horse's back, is incorrect, and the fact that the horse's forelegs and shoulders are, by Nature's design, supports and shock-absorbers, should not be forgotten. The spinal column bridging the distance between his hips and shoulders bears less strain, with consequent less fatigue, if the rider's weight is near the front of this bridge, — in other words, close to the shoulders.

---

[7] Cantle. Rear part of saddle, including back portion of seat.

Hence, the hunting man should ride with fairly short stirrups, but longer than those used in steeple-chasing.

In hacking, since the distances ridden are usually not great, and the time on the horse's back is short, the stirrups may be adjusted primarily to suit the rider's comfort. They should be fairly long. In breaking and training a young horse, there is a marked advantage in having the stirrups quite long, since the rider's legs are then well down around his mount, where they may be employed strongly as aids in teaching the lessons at hand, and also be wrapped about him to provide security of seat in case the youngster bucks or violently plays up. No matter what the length of stirrup is, the body *is always inclined to the front*; slightly with long stirrups, and progressively farther as the stirrups become shorter.

THE NATURAL SEAT FOR ALL RIDERS

This long discussion relative to the length of stirrup-straps and inclination of the body has been given, since, except for variations in these two factors, the seat is always the same. This simplifies riding of all types to a great extent, and in addition, it may be said that *the seat to be described is an exceedingly simple and natural one.* In fact, most children, as soon as they have gained a little confidence on a horse's back, assume the correct posture instinctively. Unfortunately, their natural tendencies are often ruined under the tutelage of the ignorant grooms and unqualified riding teachers abounding in this country. Also, let it be said here that women take the correct forward seat with even more facility than do men. The old statement that women are not built to ride astride is utterly absurd. The only reason women may be at a disadvantage is because they are, more often than men, nonathletic, and therefore naturally too weak for hard riding. Otherwise, a girl or woman of fairly normal proportions can ride astride easily and naturally, and in excellent form. The female conformation in general is particularly well-adapted to the forward seat.

Sketches Showing Forward Inclination of Body Necessary to Ride in Balance

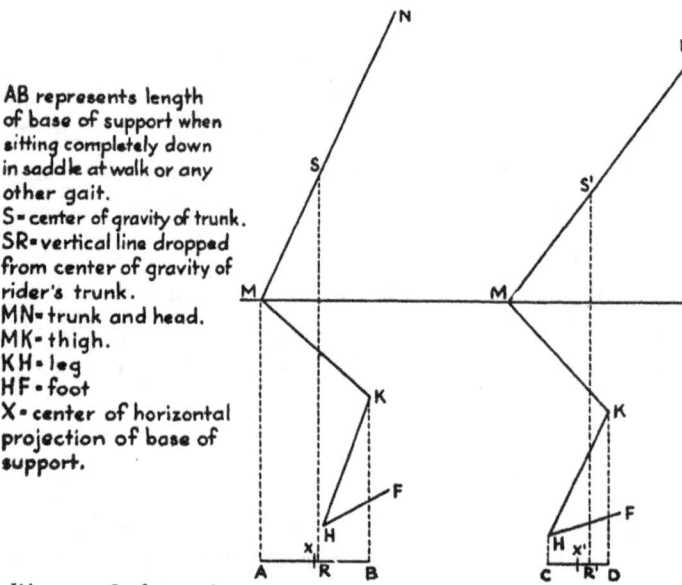

AB represents length of base of support when sitting completely down in saddle at walk or any other gait.
S = center of gravity of trunk.
SR = vertical line dropped from center of gravity of rider's trunk.
MN = trunk and head.
MK = thigh.
KH = leg
HF = foot
X = center of horizontal projection of base of support.

CD represents length of base of support when seat comes partly out of saddle at posting trot, fast gallop, during jump, or when purposely standing in stirrups at gallop.
S'R' = vertical line dropped from center of gravity of rider's trunk.
X' = center of horizontal projection of base of support.

Diagram 2 shows that at faster gaits, (posting trot or gallop), when seat is partly out of saddle much of time, trunk is inclined farther to front to be in balance over short base of support, (C - D), than when at slow gaits, (walk or canter), when rider is completely seated in saddle, and base of support is longer, (A - B), shown in Diagram 1. To compensate for body's inertia when horse is moving, center of gravity of rider's trunk should be a little in advance of center of base of support, (X and X¹). As shown diagrammatically in sketches, this is the case. S and S¹ are over R and R¹, in advance of X and X¹.

MECHANICAL ANALYSIS OF THE BALANCED SEAT

To begin with, an analysis of the seat will be undertaken from a mechanical point of view. When seated in the saddle, the rider's base of support is measured, from front to rear, by the horizontal projection of the line connecting the point where the pelvic bones rest on the saddle and the point where the inner bone of the knee is in contact with the skirt[8] of the saddle. (This distance is shown by line A-B in sketch.)

In other words, from the pelvic bone down the inner side of the thigh to and including the inside of the knee, a rider has continuous contact with the saddle *when the horse is at a walk or standing still. At the faster gaits, namely the posting trot and gallop, the rear part of the seat is slightly out of the saddle a portion of the time,* and the body's weight is on the lower thigh, knee, and in the heel of the boot. (The ankle should be relaxed so that the rider feels his weight settle in the heel, and not in the stirrup.) Consequently, the longitudinal measurement of the base of support is shortened, when the buttocks are out of the saddle, extending only from the inside of the knee to the heel

---

8 Skirt of saddle. Leather flaps which cover buckles of girths and form sides against which thighs and knees rest.

of the boot. (Shown by line C-D in sketch). Now it is perfectly evident that for the rider to keep his upper body easily in balance over its base of support, the center of gravity of all portions of the body above, and not in contact with, the saddle, must rest somewhere over the line A-B when the horse is standing or walking, or over the line C-D if the rider is posting, (rising to the trot), galloping, or jumping. These simple facts give the fundamental reason why the body, to be well-balanced in riding, must be inclined to the front. To be perfectly in balance, when the horse is moving at the walk, the center of gravity of the unstable portions of the body, — namely, the trunk, arms, and head, — should be slightly in advance of X, the center of the line A-B, since the reactions of the horse's forward movement tend to leave the rider's trunk to the rear, as a result of its inertia. Hence, at the posting trot, or fast gallop, when the buttocks come out of the saddle, — as they should, — at each stride, the trunk must be inclined forward from the hips farther than at the walk, so that the perpendicular line dropped from the center of gravity of the rider's trunk falls constantly a trifle in advance of the point X, which represents the center of his base of support, (C-D.)

A person riding without inclining the trunk to the front can, of course, stay on a horse quite successfully.

However, at each sudden or unexpected movement of his mount, such a rider's body leans perforce to the rear, crushingly weighting the horse's loin, and hindering his efforts. In the case of a very good rider, balance is recovered by gripping a little tighter with the calves of the legs, and straightening the body up toward the front. The average or poor rider, on the other hand, hangs on to the reins to maintain his equilibrium, and in so doing, gives his horse an unnecessary, brutal, and confusing jerk on the mouth when he pulls himself forward to recover his balance and regain his original position. To detail the ultimate ruinous results to the horse's mouth and disposition is superfluous. Also, a man who leans backward and constantly has Recourse to the reins in maintaining his position and balance, fails to talk an intelligent language to his horse. There is no possibility of the horse's associating the ideas of halting, turning, and decreasing the gait with tension on the reins, if it is applied hundreds of times when the rider means none of those things.

The man who rides in perfect balance, does so by maintaining a factor of safety through having sufficient forward inclination to prevent his body's being thrown out of balance to the rear by any unexpected forward movement of the horse. Consequently, he will have better hands, and his signals communicated to the horse by the reins will not be interspersed with a lot of unintentional, meaningless jerks on the mouth. As will be more fully described later, the rider should always keep his trunk more or less in front of the vertical, even when halting the horse. This prevents lugging on the reins with *unnecessary force*, as is the case with a rider who habitually leans backward and *throws his body's weight* on the reins to decrease the gait or halt. The rider who is in balance when slowing the pace or halting, employs *only his finger, wrist, and arm muscles*, the force of which can be measured nicely.

The Seat and the Saddle Needed

Great attention must everlastingly be given to one's seat. Bad habits are easily contracted, even by experienced, good riders, and just as in all other sports, when "good form" begins to fall off, your whole game goes wrong. There is a logical manner of assuming the correct seat, and if constantly followed, bad habits may be avoided.

First of all, the seat itself, — in other words, *the place in the saddle and the parts of the anatomy which are actually in contact with it,* — must be very definitely understood. *The crotch should be in the deepest part of the saddle; the pelvic bones rest lightly and squarely on the broad part of the cantle, while the fleshy part of the buttocks is well to the rear, above the saddle, and not used as a seat.* In rising to the trot, galloping, and jumping, the buttocks are oftentimes entirely out of the saddle and thrust backward, by hollowing out the loin, to serve as a counterweight for the head, arms, and trunk, which are to the front, due to the forward inclination from the hips. The center of gravity of the whole mass is approximately over the knees, (as shown by Diagram A). Since women are heavier than men about the hips, it is easier for them to maintain their balance with the forward seat, than for the latter, who, due to their conformation, are normally top-heavy. It may be added that a woman's center of gravity is also closer to the horse, which increases the stability of her seat.

Unfortunately, for many years our Army officers and troopers were taught to ride with the buttocks pushed under them, so that they were seated on the ends of their spines, with the loins convex to the rear. This faulty seat curved and humped their backs in a most ungraceful, unsightly, and "back of the horse" position. The position still largely persists in the Army, and is often seen among civilian riders. It is weak and does not allow the rider to get deeply into the saddle. In addition, it has many other attendant disadvantages which will be mentioned from time to time. The seat resembles, to some extent, what is called "the old English hunting seat," and, to modern experienced horsemen is nothing short of grotesque.

To have the narrowest part of the saddle, — the throat, as it is called, — well up in the crotch of the legs, and to keep the buttocks to the rear, necessitates having a saddle with a properly shaped seat. Many saddles are so abominably constructed that one must confine all his efforts to avoid

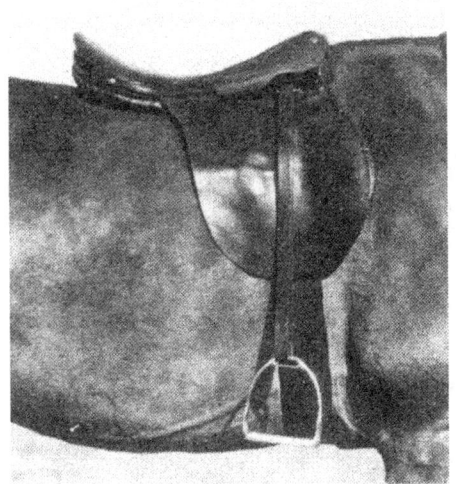

Plate X *Saumur type of saddle. Central point is lowest and near to horse's back. A comfortable and deep seat.*

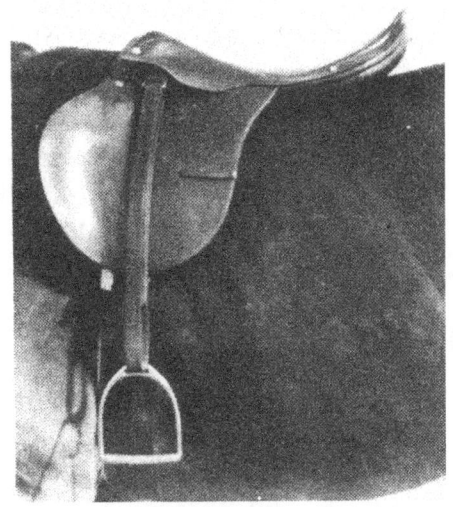

Plate XI *Italian saddle. Skirts cut farther to front than French (Saumur) saddle. Better suited for riding with very short stirrups. Excellent type for fast cross-country work and jumping high obstacles.*

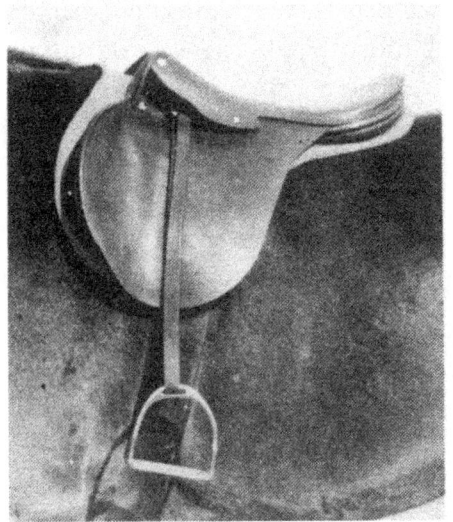

Plate XII *Polish saddle. Knee rolls similar to Italian saddle, but is somewhat broader and longer. Tall men need plenty of length when riding with long stirrups.*

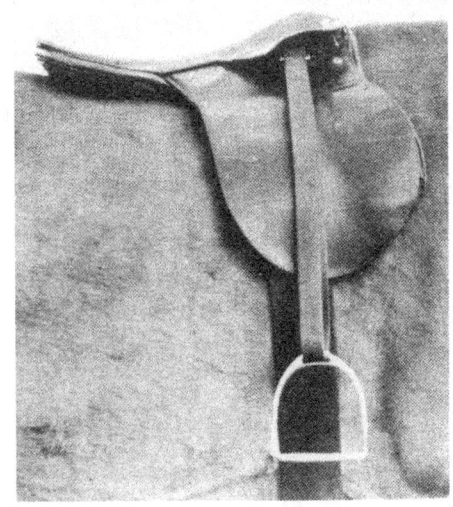

Plate XIII *Poorly-constructed saddle; lowest point at cantle.*

slipping off the cantle, and the chance of acquiring a secure, comfortable, and excellent position is impossible. The throat should be slightly in front of the center of the saddle, and should, be its lowest point, closest to the horse's back. The French Saumur saddles, or similar models, have deep, narrow-throated seats, and are excellent for beginners. The skirts[9] are cut down rather straight, and therefore are not well-adapted to riding with very short stirrups, but beginners should not ride with short stirrups.

The Italian and Polish saddles have skirts cut well out to the front, and are suitable for cross-country riding, and for show-jumping, where high obstacles are to be met. Any of the above models can be used for hunting, according to individual preference. They all have well shaped seats, whereas many saddles, while beautifully made as to workmanship, are constructed for "the old English hunting seat, " where the rider sits on the cantle, leans to the rear, and counterbalances his trunk by thrusting the feet well to the front. Several of our own saddle-makers now either import or copy the best foreign models. So, if beginning, or if one is eager to improve his riding by acquiring good form, he should first of all obtain a properly shaped saddle. Oftentimes a good saddler can pad the panels[10] of one too low behind, so as to raise the cantle a trifle, and make the throat the lowest part of the seat, which will improve it greatly. Occasionally a saddle is exaggeratedly high at the cantle, which makes the rider slip too far forward. Of course the type used on most Kentucky saddle-horses is a monstrosity, as far as being suited to any practical riding or horsemanship. Unfortunately many children are started out on such contraptions.

Thus, to recapitulate, a saddle with a properly shaped seat, should be procured; pommel-arch high enough to leave clearance over the withers of a well shaped horse, and with the cantle also high enough to eliminate all tendency, when riding, to slip backward off the saddle. The saddle must never touch any part of the horse's backbone which is only protected by the skin and hair covering it, and consequently can be easily and seriously abraded and bruised. The throat should rest close to, without touching, the back of the horse. As stated, one should not sit far forward in the seat, but should be certain that the saddle throat is deep up in the crotch, and that the pelvic bones are back on the broad part of the cantle, the buttocks behind, and not serving as a seat. The position of the trunk should, in general, be that of a person sitting upright on a chair, leaning forward just slightly, as when keenly interested in a horse race.

---

[9] Compare front edge of skirts of Saumur type of saddle with those of Italian model.

[10] Panels. Padded uderportions of saddle tree, whic rest on horse's back.

Plate XIV *Correct position of knees, legs, and heels when using short stirrups.*

Of course, a horse very high at the withers needs a saddle relatively high at the cantle, while a horse very high in the hind quarters is more agreeable to ride with a saddle a little lower at the cantle.

Stirrups and Legs

After placing the seat in the saddle, the next concern is the position of the legs. Their position will be affected by the length of the stirrup-straps. These are adjusted in length according to the type of riding to be undertaken. For hacking and normal training of the horse, when he is not to be schooled in jumping, the rule for the length of stirrup-straps is as follows: *Being seated as described above, with the legs hanging down in a natural position by the horse's sides and the feet out of the stirrups, the treads[11] of the stirrups should hang even with the center of the large bones on the inner sides of the ankle joints.* This is a general rule. One may need the stirrups a little longer or shorter, depending on his conformation, and on that of the horse. With a fat horse, for example, he will find that he can ride comfortably with a somewhat longer stirrup than when astride a "slab-sided" and very thin one. The fat one fits into the legs, whereas the thin one does not.

For a beginner, it is well to have the stirrups a little on the long side, rather than too short, as this permits, and almost forces the rider to work

---

[11] Treads. Bottoms of stirrups, on which feet rest.

the thighs and knees well down around the horse, and thus overcome the usual instinctive tendency to raise the knees, which makes the seat unstable and weakens the grip of the knees and calves. It is the ability to grip with the calves of the legs, and to a much lesser extent with the knees and thighs, that provides the strength of seat through which a good rider stays with his horse when difficulties, such as shying, kicking, plunging, stumbling, bucking or jumping arise. No matter how much the stirrups are shortened, it must be understood that the *stirrup-straps, when the seat is correct, always remain vertical, and that as a result of shorter stirrups, the knees, though raised, go very little farther to the front.* In general, they rest somewhat toward the front of the saddle skirt, but never at the front edge or beyond. On the other hand, *as the stirrups are shortened, the seat and buttocks are necessarily pushed, farther back on the cantle. This demands more forward inclination of the body from the hips, in order that the rider may remain in balance, over the center of his base of support, which is lengthened by shortening the stirrups.*

Correct Seat Easiest to Learn

The natural, balanced seat is by far the easiest to learn, and with a little practice, the average individual can soon acquire it. It has the advantages of security and comfort, and greatly favors all efforts of the horse through being mechanically correct. It will seem fatiguing at first to a person who has ridden in a different fashion for years, but after having used it for a time, other things being equal, both he and his horse will outlast and outdo men and horses, when the latter are ridden otherwise. The rider's loin will tire during first lessons from being held slightly swayed and from the forward inclination, but this will not last long, and^ he will soon be secure and comparatively tireless as he learns to ride "*forward*" and "*in form.*"

Position of Foot in Stirrup

After the stirrup has been adjusted so that the tread strikes the ankle bone, *the foot is placed well home, so that the tread rests under the instep, and not against the ball of the foot.* The almost universal habit of putting the ball of the foot on the tread is very faulty, and should only be done in schooling of a technical order, such as high-school[12] work and early training of a colt, where light touches of the spur are frequently needed. For cross-country work, polo, jumping, and other real riding, the foot belongs well home in the stirrup where it will not jar out at the least mishap, and endanger or momentarily incapacitate the rider. Moreover, unless the foot is pushed

---

12 High-school. See note on page 4, "*haute école.*"

home, it is much more difficult to keep the proper position of the heel, ankle, and leg from the knee down, which is of fundamental importance in riding correctly.

Heels

After putting the feet in the stirrups, *the ankle joints should remain relaxed, and the heels be forced down as far as possible. The importance of keeping the heels down cannot be too greatly emphasized.* It produces the strength and stability of the whole seat. With heels thus placed, the calf muscles can be powerfully contracted when it is desired to grip the horse, either to drive him forward, or to keep the seat when balance has been disturbed from any cause. With the toes lower than the heels, it is physically impossible to contract the calf muscles and grip tightly. Also, the lower legs should continuously rest against the horse's sides. *With properly adjusted stirrups, and the heels forced down as far as they will go, the calves of the legs just below the knees are forced against the horse automatically.* The ankle joints must be habitually relaxed. This in conjunction with the slight inclination of the body to the front, which forces some weight constantly into the stirrups, make it simple and natural to keep the heels down. The stirrups should be short enough so that, with the heels down, the calves of the legs can, with ease, be kept snugly against the horse's sides. If the straps are too long, the calves do not rest against the horse, the heels come up, and the whole seat is less steady, stable, and comfortable.

Feet

The toes turn out at an angle which is comfortable, and which allows the calves of the legs, particularly the inner portion just below the knees, to close against the horse. The feet will usually form an angle of between twenty and forty-five degrees with the longer axis of the horse. This angle varies slightly with the length of stirrup-straps, as well as with the conformation of the horse and rider.

Manner of Taking Seat

An excellent way to take the correct seat is, first: — place one hand on the pommel of the saddle to steady one's self, and stand in the stirrups, completely out of the saddle. The body leans forward slightly while standing in the stirrups. Next, relax the ankle joints so that the heels, driven by the body's weight, are forced far down, at the same time taking care that the stirrup-straps are *vertical*, and that the lower legs are fixed in place against the horse's sides. (See illustrations XV & XVI.) The legs should not be allowed to change position during the rest of the procedure of taking the seat. Allow the toes to turn out naturally so that the calves come automatically against the horse's sides. Then, *holding the lower legs in place with the knees fixed against the saddle,* let the seat down into the saddle by flexing the knee joints and leaning forward from the hips at the same time, so as to place the buttocks far to the rear over the cantle. This will put the crotch in the middle, or throat, of the saddle. Straighten up the body from the hips until seated in a natural and erect position. There should be a very slight forward inclination from the hips, which distributes part of the weight of the body and legs down the thighs, through the relaxed ankles and knees, into the greatly depressed heels.

The above manner of taking the seat will, as previously stated, automatically force the heels down, glue the calves of the legs to the horse, put the thighs flat against the saddle skirts, the crotch deep in the center of the saddle, and the buttocks well to the rear. The pelvic bones will then rest lightly on the saddle. The natural posture of the spine, — slightly hollowed out at the loin, — should be maintained. This and the forward inclination of the body will permit only the anterior portions of the pelvic bones to rest on the saddle. The trunk's weight will, as a result of the position, be distributed on the pelvic bones, down the thighs, and a portion will always be transmitted through the partially relaxed knees and ankles into the heels. When riding, the weight of the body borne by the heels, (through the stirrups), and in addition, that of the legs themselves, keep pushing the heels and knees down at each stride. This closes the calves against the horse if the knee joints are relaxed, makes the contact constant, and gripping with the calves, or even the knees, when necessary, very easy. The rider is in balance.

Thighs

The thighs assume the proper position without effort if the seat in the saddle is taken as has just been described. They should always cling softly to the saddle. The heavy muscles on the inner and back part of them should rest in rear of the thigh-bone, so that the thighs, throughout their length, may press flat against the saddle skirts. If the buttocks are not kept pushed to the rear, but are allowed to get forward in the center of the saddle, through having the loin con-vexed or humped, it is almost impossible to keep the thighs in correct position. *The loin, therefore, must never hump backward, but habitually be kept slightly concave, or sway-backed, just as when standing erect.* See Plate XVI This helps keep the fleshy part of the buttocks back toward the cantle, and the crotch in the throat of the saddle, and makes keeping the thighs flat automatic. Moreover, the back muscles remain under muscular control, whereas if the loin is allowed to hump and sag, the back muscles are limp, and the rider becomes a leaden-like load sitting on his spine's end, readily toppling forward or falling backward at quick moves by the horse. He becomes an inverted pendulum.

Knees

The knees rest snugly at all times against the saddle, which follows naturally if the trunk, seat, and thighs are placed as just described. *They do not grip hard except in emergencies, or to prevent the seat from slipping forward in the saddle, in case the horse slows his pace or halts abruptly.*

Gripping too tightly with the knees or thighs is fatiguing, produces general stiffness, and squeezes a rider out of his seat, just as a lemon seed can be forced out from between the thumb and forefinger by squeezing. Unfortunately it is a habit instinctive with beginners. The leg grip should be most powerful just below the knees, and is produced by the calves. The knees also tighten, however, to hold the seat in place if the horse pulls, or when much tension is required on the reins. The brace of the feet against the stirrups, (due to the very low position of the heels), assisted by the pressure of the knees when necessary, permits a rider to maintain the forward inclination of the body and hold his seat in place while restraining a pulling horse. Also, in case the horse stumbles, "pecks" in front of a jump, or stops unexpectedly, the grip of the knees increases to help keep the seat fixed in place. It is vital in all these cases, that the back be kept naturally straight, and not humped over, in order to keep from falling forward. *Always, the body is inclined forward from the hips.* The inclination is just sufficient to keep a portion of the weight distributed down the thighs and into the stirrups, and should be no greater, as the position then becomes ungraceful and unstable. If the knees have a tendency to rise, the rider is leaning to the rear, out of balance, and is "behind the horse."

A common fault always to be guarded against, is stiffening the knee joints. Only when purposely standing in the stirrups should this be done. This will be discussed later. Normally, the knee joints are almost completely relaxed. They are not entirely limp, but work sufficiently to keep the lower legs in place. If the joints are absolutely limp, the lower legs slip too far to the rear, which permits the heels to come up, the buttocks to slide forward, and the strength and balance of the whole seat to be destroyed.

Plate XV *Standing in stirrups to force heels down before taking seat. Rider should be able to assume this position at any gait, without first increasing inclination of the body, if he is riding in balance.*

Plate XVI *Rider seated after standing in stirrups, buttocks to rear, body inclined to front, in correct position at halt or walk.*

Head

It is highly important to keep the head and chin up. The chest is also lifted to give the sensation of the whole spine's being stretched upward, — in short, there should be a feeling of making one's self tall. This will give the "feel" of riding "lightly." This position and manner of carrying the body then *aids* the horse in all his movements, and helps keep him contented by facilitating his work. It prevents ruining his mouth by jerks devoid of meaning, such as a person leaning backward involuntarily administers.

Everyone knows what an enormous effort is required to lift a person who allows his body to remain perfectly relaxed and limp. For the same reason, it is /most tiring work *for a horse* to carry a rider who collapses in the saddle like a sack of sand. In addition, such riding is unsightly and fatiguing.

Loin

The body, although held upright, should be devoid of stiffness and rigidity. The loin functions as a spring which takes up much of the jar due to the reactions of the horse's movements. It must remain in a natural position, just as when standing erect, so that it can give in a supple manner either to the front or rear. It should be constantly under voluntary muscular control, *partially relaxed, but not collapsed,* as is often erroneously taught. The hip, knee, and ankle joints, together with the loin, absorb and soften the jars resulting from the horse's movements.

Shoulders and Arms

The shoulders should be carried squarely. The instinct in beginners to tighten the shoulder muscles must be overcome. The upper arms hang naturally from relaxed shoulder joints, and the body's forward inclination allows the elbows to fall slightly in front of it, when the reins are properly adjusted. Always there should be a pronounced bend at the elbows, and *the play of the elbow joints is vastly important in acquiring good hands.* All the muscles of the arms and hands, as well as those of the wrists, elbows, and shoulders, should, except when tension is purposely applied to the reins, be almost completely relaxed. When the horse is going quietly, and the reins are not being used to affect his gait or direction, only enough muscular effort is exerted to keep the forearms raised and the elbow joints softly flexed. This will be more fully discussed under the subject of hands in a later chapter.

The Seat Summarized

The following rules for the positions of the various parts of the body are given to summarize the preceding discussion for the purpose of ready reference. It is advisable to study carefully the lengthy descriptions given heretofore, for, while the seat is in no way difficult, in order to secure perfect form, it is absolutely essential that all parts of the body assume correct positions. Any faulty attitude of one part inevitably provokes repercussions on others, and throws the whole out of adjustment. Studying the accompanying illustrations and diagrams will aid greatly in fully comprehending the details of the seat, and with these in mind, practice will do the rest.

1. **Pelvic Bones**: anterior parts rest evenly on saddle; crotch in throat of saddle; fleshy part of buttocks well to rear, and must not be allowed to slip forward under rider.

2. **Thighs**: flat; heavy muscles to rear of femur; continuous contact down to, and including inner sides of knees.

3. **Knees**: inside of knee bones against saddle skirts; kept as low as possible, with stirrup-straps vertical; not allowed to turn too far outward, leaving air space between them and saddle; normally do not grip tightly, — just sufficiently to keep whole thigh softly against saddle skirts. Knee joints almost completely relaxed, except when purposely standing in stirrups; knees increase grip when necessary to keep seat from being displaced forward or sideways from any cause; must not be entirely limp, or lower legs slip to rear, and heels come up.

4. **Lower Legs**: inner and upper portion of calves always in soft contact with sides of horse; no great effort required to keep them there. Calves squeeze to drive horse ahead, and to maintain the seat in case of emergency, due to unexpected movement of horse. Position of lower legs automatically correct when stirrup-straps are vertical, and heels thrust down to absolute limit, with ankle joints relaxed. *Heels kept down* when squeezing or gripping with calves.

5. **Ankles**: habitually relaxed, allowing weight transmitted down thighs through partially relaxed knees to sink into heels of boots.

6. **Feet**: turned out so that upper, inner sides of calves rest against horse. Toes make angle of twenty to forty-five degrees with longitudinal axis of horse. Feet home in stirrups. No effort ever made to turn outer edge of feet upward, as this stiffens ankles, and throws calves away from horse's sides.

7. **Heels**: thrust far down. Give brace, if horse checks suddenly, so seat does not slip forward.

Plate XVII *Incorrect seat. Heels not sufficietly depressed; knees too far forward and too high; weight concentrated on cantle; loin and back humped; chest and head not lifted; reins too long.*

Plate XVIII *Correct seat with normal length of stirrup-straps. Heels and knees forced well down; calves in close contact with horse; body inclined forward, distributing weight down thighs and in stirrups; loin and trunk erect; chest and head lifted. Compare with Plate XVII.*

8. **Trunk and Spine**: carried in same posture as when standing very erect. Whole trunk inclined to front *from hips. Center of gravity of trunk rests over point in front of pelvic bones at halt, walk, or very slow gaits, when fully seated in saddle. At fast trot or gallop, center of gravity is approximately over knees.* Loin habitually swayed in normal, natural position; never remains convex to rear.

9. **Chest, Head and Chin**: lifted. Whole body carried lightly.

THE SEAT

Three Important Points

As knee joints stiffen a trifle to aid brace of feet against stirrups when horse checks suddenly, knees also grip saddle more tightly, and back muscles stiffen momentarily to keep spine swayed slightly, which prevent body's toppling forward. All this is natural after practice, and prevents buttocks slipping forward, and lower legs going to rear, which disrupts whole seat, involving surrender of balance, and control of horse. *If heels are thrust down and back is kept swayed, balance and forward inclination of body can be easily maintained under difficulties.*

Fortunately, knees, when properly placed, are approximately in the transverse vertical plane containing horse's center of gravity, when standing still. Hence, with this seat, center of gravity of horse and rider fall approximately in same vertical line.

Stiffness should be avoided. As much relaxation should exist throughout whole anatomy as is consistent with maintaining muscular control of the body, balance, and the seat steadily in place.

CHAPTER II

HOW TO LEARN AND RIDE THE FORWARD SEAT

Progress in learning to ride or improving your seat is most rapid when a logical step-by-step system is followed. Unfortunately, riding is usually first undertaken without theoretical knowledge, plan, or method. But even in this haphazard manner strong seats are developed. A strong seat, however, is not synonymous with a good seat, nor does it presuppose riding in "good form." Many riders are securely seated in their saddles regardless of the defenses or violent actions of their horses, simply because they have spent many hours riding many different mounts. Nevertheless, these same riders lack the skill, finish, and ability of those who have learned to ride in good form through methodical instruction, study and practice. Of course, the riding of the latter is more successful in the field and in competition, since good form in any sport always produces the best results.

There are *four prime elements* which a beginner should first acquire, in the following sequence.

1. *He must gain confidence on his horse.* This is inspired by riding, during early lessons, only very docile, well-trained mounts with good gaits and manners. By no means should a novice ever start out on a difficult, nervous, or flighty horse. Many enthusiasts, especially women, commencing bravely enough, have become terribly frightened and never regained confidence, through having been first mounted on unmanageable or high-strung horses which ran away with or unseated them. Beginners have neither the security of seat nor the knowledge necessary to control such horses.

2. Beginners, and oftentimes riders of experience, having acquired confidence on the horse, next must learn mental and muscular relaxation. Instinctive apprehension to begin with, and later the bad habits resulting from this apprehension, cause many to ride with various muscles habitually contracted. This muscular contraction may be in the shoulders, legs, body, or elsewhere, but general stiffness and awkwardness follow, and make

comfortable, graceful riding impossible. Having a quiet horse on which the tyro quickly gains confidence will also greatly hasten relaxation. The practice of certain "suppling exercises," to be described later in this chapter, will, however, furnish the surest means of producing general relaxation.

3. When confidence and relaxation have been fairly well established, the time is at hand to develop security of seat. The most important feature in this third step is *sitting correctly in the saddle*. The exact positions of the legs, trunk, arms and hands are not stressed; only that of the seat in the saddle is dealt with in this phase. The exercise par excellence for developing security of seat is riding without stirrups, also described later in this chapter.

4. *Keeping the hands quiet and soft*, thus avoiding pain to the horse's mouth, is the fourth fundamental. From the first lesson, it must be realized that good horsemanship hinges on not abusing the mouth through unconscious, but nevertheless painful jerks caused by bobbing, jumpy hands and an unsteady seat.

In this connection, there are many riders of experience who continually, though unknowingly, punish their horses' mouths by unnecessary jerking and pulling. Unfortunately, they are not only blissfully unaware of their shortcomings, but are usually of the type who secretly pride themselves on their "good hands."

Be sure that the steps just enumerated are taken in the following order:

1. *Confidence,*
2. *Relaxation,*
3. *Good Seat in the Saddle,*
4. *Quiet Hands, and Constant Regard for the Horse's Mouth.*

When these requisites of primary equitation are learned, the basic foundation from which to scale the heights of horsemanship is properly laid.

Before going into detail on the method to be pursued in practice to cover the four desiderata above, it should be stated that whenever possible, the services of a qualified instructor should be obtained. Unfortunately there is a dearth of this type in the United States. If a good one is not available, two people may work together with great success. By mutual advice and criticism, with concurrent study of the illustrations and descriptions of the seat, hands, etc., both can quickly improve their riding. Moreover, various points which arise involving a difference of opinion will ultimately be correctly settled, where two may argue the matter out.

Most of the best international riders, — particularly if they feel themselves becoming "stale" or "out of form," — habitually seek the opinions and criticisms of their comrades. No one ever learns all there is to know about either horses or riding. Hence the wise horseman is always trying to gain knowledge from others. If properly modest, you will soon discover that every groom or stable-boy usually has at least one new bit of information to impart. Of course these bits must be filtered through the sieve of common sense to separate the genuine from the humbug, — the latter being notoriously prevalent in stable lore. Strangely enough, many people with two or three years' riding experience, — oftentimes less, — feel that there is nothing more for them to learn; that a cloak of equestrian omniscience has fallen on their shoulders. Then too, as Mr. Jorrocks so aptly remarked: many a young man would rather have an "h'imputation on 'is morality than on 'is 'ossmanship." Needless to say, these riders never reach the top flight. One must always keep an open mind and know that there is always more to learn.

"Practice makes perfect" in riding as in all else, providing, of course, that correct principles and proper methods are pursued. Ride much, and as many horses as possible. All are different. Each horse must be studied as an individual. In applying to many horses the broad principles of training to be given, your methods must of necessity vary somewhat, and through learning to select the correct method for each case, your tact and skill will grow. At all the cavalry schools, the officers interchange horses approximately every three days, so that each rides a hundred or more during the year's instruction. Manifestly the object of this is to teach the officers "equestrian tact," which means the ability, first, to analyze each horse's temperament, faults and defenses; second, to adopt suitable methods in training and riding in order gradually to dominate and control him.

Be certain to obtain a good saddle, with the throat in the deepest part. Above all, avoid one with a low cantle, which causes you to slip backward on it. (See illustrations of suitable types of French, Italian, and American saddles in Chapter I.) For those just learning to ride, the French Saumur, or similar models, are perhaps the best, as they are well adapted to using fairly long stirrups. Also, they have deep seats, which not only give a feeling of security, but as a matter of fact actually do aid one in maintaining balance. In early lessons the stirrup-straps should be "on the long side, " since the rider is then forced to keep the thighs and knees well down around the horse, thus overcoming the beginner's tendency to raise the knees.

I. Gaining Confidence

The beginner, on a sweet-tempered, well-trained horse, should for the first few days go with the instructor, (or if working in pairs, with his friend, also on a calm and steady mount), for quiet promenades out-of-doors. The gait should be slow, only the walk being undertaken for the first one or two lessons, and the lessons should not be of such long duration as to cause muscle stiffness and soreness. Remember that this is the period primarily devoted to instilling confidence, and while minor corrections and words of assistance concerning the seat and hands can be given from time to time, harassing a novice with many detailed corrections before he has completely lost all apprehension and stiffness, should be carefully avoided. The rider should be made to forget the horse, to talk, laugh and enjoy the ride, and thus unconsciously lose all fear.

II. Relaxation

The suppling exercises, previously mentioned and to be described later, can normally be initiated about the third lesson. Their specific purpose is to insure relaxation. They have been successfully employed at the American and French Cavalry Schools for many years. In addition to increasing the rider's confidence and ability to stay on his horse *through producing relaxation*, they have the important objective of developing "independence of the aids."

Independence of the Aids

The "aids" consist of the rider's hands (reins), legs, spurs, voice, weight, and occasionally the whip. Possessing independence of the aids means that a rider is sufficiently skillful to use, for example, his right rein in turning a horse to the right, and at the same time his right leg (or spur, if need be) to push the horse's haunches to the left in order to hasten the turn. If his independence in the use of the aids is perfect, his left rein and left leg will make no unintentional movements of any sort while he is employing the right rein and right leg. They should remain completely quiet and passive.

A finished rider can use both hands and both legs simultaneously, each one doing a totally different thing in controlling a horse which is unruly and violent in his defenses, or for the purpose of demanding a certain movement. Naturally, perfection in independence of the aids requires much concentration and practice. The legs and hands must not only act independently of each other, but independently of the reactions of the rider's body resulting from the horse's movements. Thus, while the suppling exercises are practiced primarily to produce relaxation, they also teach independence of the aids through developing the requisite coordination and muscular control.

III. Security of Seat

As soon as quiet promenades and suppling exercises have given the rider confidence and relaxation on the horse, *security of seat* should next occupy his attention. Nothing will make a secure seat so quickly and surely as riding without stirrups. This must be started with short periods at the walk, later at a very slow trot, and finally at the canter. A strong, well-balanced seat soon results, along with suppleness and relaxation. Without a good seat good hands are never found; without both good seat and good hands there can be no independence of the aids. In turn, without independence of the aids you can never clearly express your desires to the horse.

No matter how much experience you may have had, a few minutes' jogging about without stirrups each time you ride will do much toward improving your seat. This exercise stretches out the leg muscles, settles you deep in the saddle, and gives your sense of balance a little "tuning up." Then when the feet are put back in the stirrups, you experience a new-found sense of security and balance. Many of the greatest riders never cease this practice. At most cavalry schools student officers are required to ride for several months in the riding hall, across country and over jumps without stirrups.

Needless to say, since one rides more lightly with the stirrups, it is less fatiguing to man and horse, — more particularly to the horse, — but no amount of riding with stirrups can replace the work without, insofar as producing a secure seat is concerned. Let it be reiterated, therefore, that a few minutes' riding without stirrups each day will keep the veteran's seat supple and well balanced, and be of immeasurable assistance to the beginner from all points of view.

The Seat Without Stirrups

The seat without stirrups is somewhat different from the one with stirrups, described in the preceding chapter. This difference is due to the fact that the rider's entire weight is carried in the seat of the saddle, since none can be supported in the stirrups. The knees are also lower, and consequently farther to the rear on the saddle skirt. Neither the knee nor ankle joints can function as shock-absorbers, as they both do with the feet in the stirrups. The body must therefore be carried more nearly vertical, and inclined only slightly to the front, for the rider's base of support without stirrups is very short. At the walk and slow trot the inclination is very slight, the trunk being almost vertical; while at the canter the inclination is a trifle more pronounced. Too much forward inclination when riding without stirrups causes the rider to be perched precariously and uncomfortably "on the fork."

Plate XIX *Seat without stirrups.*

The legs are allowed to hang in a natural manner, and the rider sits on the pelvic bones and the extreme upper, inner thighs. As has just been pointed out, the knees and lower thighs cannot aid in bearing part of the weight of the trunk, as they do when stirrups are used, unless the rider pinches too hard with his knees, which is a very bad though quite common fault. If the knees and thighs are raised as a result of leaning backward, the seat is weak and insecure, and the rider is out of balance to the rear. The thighs should be allowed to slope naturally forward and downward, and as with stirrups, should be in continuous contact with the saddle, down to and including the back part of the large bones on the inside of the knee joints. The knees are kept turned inward, but without exerting enough muscular effort to pinch hard. They are not turned in so far that the calf and lower leg are thrown away from the horse's sides.

The large inner thigh muscles should rest back of the thigh bones, so that the thighs are "flat" against the saddle-skirts, which is impossible if the knees turn limply outward. When the horse is in motion, the lower legs — specifically the upper, inner portions of the calves — are kept gently closed against the horse's sides by flexing the knee joints until the calves gain soft contact. The calves grip tightly only when necessary in order to maintain one's seat, because of violent or unexpected movements by the horse. An effort must usually be made by beginners to keep the thighs, knees and lower legs well down around the horse. Carefully avoid raising the knees. The ankle joints are relaxed, and the absence of stirrups permits the toes to hang downward. In emergencies the toes are raised in order to contract the calf muscles, which permits gripping tightly. Head, chest and eyes are kept raised. Allowing the head to hang forward and watching the horse's neck will inevitably destroy the whole seat. The loin (lower part of back) and hip joints must be supple in order to absorb the jars resulting from the slow trot and canter. The loin is held naturally, and not humped to the rear, which produces slouching and puts the rider out of balance.

A beginner, during first lessons without stirrups, should continuously hold the saddle pommel or the neck strap of a martingale[13] with one hand, and the reins with the other, especially when work at the trot and canter is first begun. Lessons at first should be very short, and the student must frequently grasp the pommel to readjust and correct his position, as well as to steady his seat, even after he rides quite well, for the horse's movements at rapid gaits make maintenance of the correct position difficult.

It is well to start the lessons in a riding hall or fenced arena, as the enclosure makes it easy to guide and control the horse.

At the earliest possible opportunity, "suppling exercises" — *previously begun while riding with stirrups* — should be executed while riding without them. A few of these are described here merely as examples. Many others can be improvised, and all are beneficial in increasing confidence, relaxation, independence of the aids, security and balance in the saddle.

Suppling Exercises

EXERCISE 1. At a walk, slow trot or canter, the rider describes vertical circles with the right arm, while endeavoring to keep his left hand — which is holding the reins — quiet and undisturbed despite the movements of the right arm and the body's reactions from the horse's gaits. The same is repeated with the left arm, the right hand holding the reins. At first the reins should be allowed to hang quite loose and floating to avoid jerking the horse's mouth.

EXERCISE 2. The feet, out of the stirrups, are rotated at the ankle joints, — up, — in, — down, — out.

---

[13] Martingale. Running martingale is shown in Plate XIV. It should be adjusted so that it exerts no "pulley" effect unless the horse raises his head to an abnormally high position. It is useful to keep reins from flapping. No martingale will lower a "star-gazer's" head; "educated hands" furnish the only cure. See page 80, Chapter IV. The strap about the neck on a martingale is often useful to hold onto when climbing steep hills and indifficulties, to avoid pulling on the horse's mouth.

EXERCISE 3. The legs are flexed back and forth alternately at the knee. The insides of the knees and the thighs remain clinging softly but firmly in place against the saddle, only the lower legs moving.

EXERCISE 4. Exercises 2 and 3 are combined with the rotations of one of the arms (given in Exercise 1). Meanwhile, the seat should be fixed and steady, and as stated, the thighs and knees should be held still in their proper positions. The rein hand should remain quiet. Either hand may hold the reins in any of the exercises.

EXERCISE 5. One arm is extended horizontally to the side, palm upward, and describes horizontal arcs by twisting *the body* from right to left and back. *All movement is at the waist,* the head turning with the body, the seat in the saddle and the legs remaining undisturbed.

EXERCISE 6. The shoulders are rotated forward, upward, backward, and down.

EXERCISE 7. The head is turned to the right and left, bent forward and back, etc.

Any of the above exercises may be combined as the rider becomes adept.

As soon as the student becomes expert enough to keep the reins constantly stretched, the contact with the horse's mouth should be continuously maintained with unchanging intensity *through the flexibility of the elbow joints.* Skill and elasticity in the fingers and wrists also aid the elbows in making "good hands."

After the rider feels "at home" on the horse, great security of seat may be developed by riding over a series of very small jumps, (from one and a half to three feet in height), without stirrups and without reins. Facilities for such work should be arranged in an enclosure. It must be understood that this is not for the purpose of acquiring a cross-country or jumping seat, but is simply an exercise to give security and balance. Starting with one small obstacle, later on four, five or six may be set up, about twenty-two feet apart, and enclosed in a chute. Some of the suppling exercises just described should be executed while going over these jumps, thus teaching independence of the seat as regards any movements of the hands, legs, head or body. Of course a quiet, steady horse is needed, and the jumping is started only after the rider is quite secure of seat.

One may learn to ride well without doing any of these exercises, yet when practiced, they are not only extremely helpful to good riding, but are amusing and greatly shorten the time required to learn. More important still, they develop that perfect coordination which is absolutely essential to high-class riding.

IV. Quiet Hands

When confidence, relaxation and a fairly secure seat are established, *the beginner should next bend all efforts toward keeping the hands quiet while maintaining a steady, light feel on the reins.*

As mentioned previously, until the seat is steady and the rider confident and relaxed, it is absolutely impossible to have "good hands." The old adage, "No seat — no hands, " is indeed true. At this stage of instruction, however, quietness of hands, not finesse in the use of them, is taught. The beginner should at first ride with loose, floating reins, and little by little he must learn to keep continuous, light and unvarying tension on the bit, with reins stretched softly taut. Of course, periods of rest with a loose rein are frequently given the horse. The rider should never support his weight or maintain his balance through leaning backward and pulling on the reins.

The suppling exercises, — which are executed with a loose, floating rein to begin with, — will gradually develop enough independence of the aids and relaxation so that the rider can *keep the hands steady and quiet through the flexibility and play of the shoulder, elbow, wrist and finger joints. These joints must be almost completely relaxed when the horse is going quietly at the desired rate and gait.* The elbows particularly should be very flexible. To obtain this, they are always held partly bent. Straightened, stiff arms with tightly clenched fingers give poor hands. As-the rider's body moves from the reactions of the horse's gait, the elbow joints open and close sufficiently to keep the reins stretched and the hands steady and apparently quiet. While the hands follow the movements of the horse's head at the walk and canter, they should not bob up and down, or spasmodically jerk his mouth. Hands that can keep the reins softly stretched, with no jerking or variation in tension, are aptly termed by James Fillis[14] "good hands." They are not necessarily educated or skillful hands. "Good hands" must be developed first; skillful, educated ones come later. It is not difficult to educate "good hands, " but poor hands can never be educated.

Starting with his first lesson, a beginner should always bear in mind the sensitiveness and feelings of his horse's mouth. He will avoid jerking it at first only by riding with a loose rein. As he gains security of seat and skill, ability to keep the reins stretched with light, unvarying tension will gradually develop. This constant contact with the horse's mouth is the principal means of talking to him. Hands and their technique will be more fully discussed in a later chapter.

---

[14] James Fillis. A celebrated and brilliant high-school rider; at one time Ecuyer en Chef at the St. Petersburg Cavalry School.

METHOD IN LEARNING TO RIDE

Once more, let it be urged that in learning to ride or improving your seat and form, you be methodical. After acquiring, in order, (1) confidence, (2) relaxation, (3) fairly secure seat, and (4) quiet hands that do not bob about and jerk the horse's mouth at each stride, by a similar step-by-step progression you concentrate on perfecting the details of your position. Thus far, only in the last of the four fundamentals cited above has the seat been touched upon, and this only concerned the actual seat in the saddle. It being established, the legs, arms, trunk, feet, etc., must next be correctly placed. A large mirror in a riding hall is a great assistance in checking the errors in one's own position at this stage.

Attack the problem of correcting details of the seat in the order given in Chapter I, "The Seat." Do not try to master all at once, but study and perfect one point at a time, consulting Chapter I frequently. The correct sequence is as follows: Position of:

1. Seat in saddle.
2. Thighs and knees.
3. Lower legs.
4. Ankles, heels and feet.
5. Loin and back.
6. Chest and head.
7. Arms, elbows and hands.

In taking the correct seat, any faulty attitude of one part of the anatomy immediately affects others. Therefore, criticisms and general instructions concerning the seat as a whole must, of necessity be given from time to time. However, concentrating on each part individually and in the order given above will insure the best results. Corrections relating to some part, not being stressed at the moment, should only be made when the incorrect position of that part adversely affects the seat as a whole. For example: although the seat in the saddle is the first detail taught, it may be that the rider's back is so humped and his loin so convexed to the rear that it is impossible for him to sit in the saddle correctly. In such a case, he must be directed to straighten the back and loin so that the proper seat can be taken.

Riding at the Walk

A pithy French axiom states, "The walk is the mother of the gaits." Work at the walk is indeed of vast benefit to both horse and rider. Few horsemen realize its full importance in training and conditioning a horse. According to the best veterinarians, it is the only gait at which the horse gains strength and does not lose weight. In addition, *it is at a walk that a rider can best learn to take the correct seat, and at the same time apply his aids*

Plate XX *Teaching young horse a long, free striding walk. Legs active, hands soft and passive. Low head carriage and extension of neck encouraged.*

with precision. Unfortunately, it is quite common to see riders slouch in the saddle and assume the most ungraceful attitudes when the horse is walking. Almost without exception this bad habit influences the seat at the trot and gallop. Moreover, when a rider slouches at the walk, he tires his horse, because his weight is entirely concentrated on the cantle, — too far to the rear on the horse's back. See Plate XVII. Due to his conformation the horse can more easily carry his load when the bulk of it is borne on the forelegs.

When the seat is correctly taken at the walk, the body is slightly inclined to the front *from the hip joints,* so that the rider feels some of his trunk's weight pushing the thighs, knees and heels down. This sensation gives proof that the body is in the proper attitude, that the trunk is in balance, with its center of gravity *in front of the pelvic bones,* and that the weight is properly distributed on the horse's back.

Another manner of testing the correctness of your position at any gait, is to have sufficient forward inclination so that without increasing that inclination at all, you can any moment stand in your stirrups, — completely out of the saddle. See Plate XV. When standing in the stirrups, the stirrup-strap should remain vertical and the weight be supported *entirely in the heels, with ankle joints relaxed.* The knees are slightly flexed, — not completely straightened, — so that the seat, though out of the saddle, is close to it. This is the position assumed when galloping fast across country, and also during the period when the seat is completely out of the saddle while posting to the trot.

If you cannot take this position and stand in the stirrups at any time, without first leaning forward at the hips, you are "behind your horse," and should increase the inclination of the body to the front, until you can. As the heels are lower than the balls of the feet and support all the weight, — if the ankle joints are entirely relaxed, — it is absolutely necessary to lean from the hips toward the front in order to remain in balance, when standing in the stirrups. The extreme lower part of the thighs, the inside of the knees, and the calves must grip the horse somewhat more strongly in order to steady and secure the seat.

Both the appearance and the feeling of the rider when at the walk should be of *"going with the horse;"* not of leaning backward and being dragged along. The hands softly follow the horse's mouth as his head and neck move forward and back, while pressure with the calves of the legs, — or, if necessary, touches with the spur, — urge him to walk fast and freely. A bold, long-striding walk is a great asset, and can be easily cultivated in a young horse. The rider's whole body should be relaxed and comfortable, — neither stiff nor limp. He should appear erect, alert, graceful and at ease.

Riding at the Slow Trot

When sitting tight in the saddle at the trot or slow trot, (not posting[15]), the seat is exactly as described for the walk. The slow trot is at a rate of about six miles per hour, and is easy to sit, either with or without stirrups. It is an excellent gait for work without stirrups, as well as for schooling horses. The rider can be comfortably and securely seated after a little practice, and can apply the aids with exactitude. As when at the walk, the body is inclined forward from the hips *only a trifle,* so that its center of gravity is just in front of the points where the pelvic bones are in contact with the saddle. The reaction resulting from the grounding of the horse's feet at each step, should thrust the rider's knees and heels down around the horse, if the body is properly inclined to the front, and if he does not make the mistake of pinching too hard with the knees. On the other hand, if the body leans backward, the knees and heels will be constantly working upward, and the rider will be "behind his horse." As a consequence, he will be forced into the pernicious habit of pulling on the reins to maintain his balance. *The knee and hip joints must be relaxed, and the loin kept erect and pliable to absorb the jars resulting from the horse's movements.*

Tension on the reins should be light and unvarying. In this connection, it is to be noted that the faster the rate becomes, the greater becomes the tension on the reins. The well-ridden and well-trained horse first slowly learns to accept this support; later, to seek it.

---

[15] Posting. Described under next Sub-title.

Plate XXI *Posting on right diagonal. Seat in saddle as right fore and left hind strike ground.*

Plate XXII *Posting on right diagonal, seat being out of saddle as left fore and right hind strike ground. If riding in balance, rider, by stiffening knee joints, should be able to remain standing in stirrups for a stride or two. Stirrups have been shortened for jumping.*

Riding at the Normal Trot

The "normal trot" varies from about eight miles to nine and a half miles per hour, depending on the horse. During all their training, horses should be carefully schooled to take the same steady rate at the "normal trot." Only when the rider indicates by his reins or legs that he desires the "slow trot" or the "extended trot," should his horse vary from the normal one. Even with the reins hanging loose, a well-trained horse takes and maintains, calmly and steadily, the normal trot. This habit, formed by proper training, adds greatly to the pleasure and comfort of both horse and rider. The "extended trot," as the name indicates, is very fast, and is used largely for schooling purposes. Its exact rate depends entirely upon the horse's natural speed, although with all horses the speed can be greatly increased by training. Every horse should be gradually taught to extend the trot to the limit of his ability at the rider's demand. It is unexcelled as an exercise for the purpose of developing the horse's strength and teaching him to take a frank support on the bit. This fast trot should be taken only on level, soft ground, due to the chance of injuring the horse's feet or legs. *It should not be employed when riding in company.* Nothing is more discourteous or annoying to horsemen than to have some person take an absurdly fast trot when hacking[16] with a group of people. This, of course, applies as well to any other gait. Oftentimes going to or returning from hunt meets, certain offenders, — the Masters, alas, in some cases, — take a walk or trot much too slow or too fast, which results in great discomfort and inconvenience to everyone else in the group. It also develops bad habits in the horses, since they must be either constantly held back in the first case, or forced to jog or gallop to keep up, in the second. Therefore, teach your horse a walk of four miles per hour, a slow trot of six miles per hour, and a normal trot of approximately eight and a half miles per hour. The speed at the extended trot will vary with each horse.

Any true horseman is always considerate of the other man's horse. If your companion has a very young or nervous one, while your own mount is calm and well-behaved, stay a little to the rear, so as not to excite his. Even while hunting there are many opportunities to do a neighbor on a green colt a good turn, by simply riding a course which will not upset his horse.

At the normal trot the rider "posts," or "rises to the trot." In posting, the seat only comes into the saddle at every other stride. The horse's right forefoot and his left hind one are jointly called the "right diagonal;" similarly, the left fore and right hind form the "left diagonal." The feet of each diagonal strike the ground simultaneously at the trot, which therefore is

---

[16] Hacking. Quiet pleasure riding.

a gait of two beats. At the normal trot, between the grounding of alternate diagonals, there is a period when all four feet are off the ground. This is called "the period of suspension." In posting on the right diagonal, for example, a rider settles fully into the saddle as the right fore and left hind feet strike the ground. As the "right diagonal" legs extend and propel the horse forward, the rider allows himself to be thrust forward and upward, remaining out of the saddle as the "left diagonal" (left fore and right hind) strike the ground, extend and throw the mass onto the right diagonal again, as those feet are grounded. Thus he returns to the saddle each time the right diagonal is grounded. In posting on the right diagonal, the rider's weight, after being thrown upward, is received in the stirrups as the left diagonal hits the ground. The knee joints, hip joints and back muscles combine to let the rider come into the saddle *lightly and springily.*

Posting is undoubtedly easier for both mount and man. However, a rider should be careful to post half the time on one diagonal and half on the other, in order to equalize the work and development of both. If a horse becomes lame in a foot of one diagonal, the rider should post on the other diagonal, as the one on which the posting is done does much more work.

In posting, the forward inclination from the hips is very pronounced. Since the seat is out of the saddle much of the time, the rider is necessarily riding during those periods "in the stirrups," and his base of support is very short. His weight, — as he starts downward after being propelled upward and forward by the horse, — is first caught in the stirrups, as stated above, but the lower thighs just above the knees, and the inside of the knees, (which press rather snugly against the saddle when posting), also aid in steadying the seat. The calves are constantly closed against the horse's sides. They are always the principal means of securing the seat against loss of balance, when the horse's movements are violent.

It is most essential to avoid humping the back or loin when posting. The small of the back is hollowed out and kept quite stiff all the time. The body must of necessity be inclined sharply to the front from the hips, so that the rider's center of gravity may rest approximately in a vertical plane passing upward just back of his knees. In other words, he is continuously balanced over a point between his knees and heels. As the seat comes into the saddle, it is done with a soft, elastic action; not with the leaden-like thump so often seen, where a rider holds his body perpendicularly, or, still worse, leans to the rear while posting. Such an attitude leaves him entirely "behind his horse, " and in addition forces him to pound the poor creature's back at each stride, while he zealously guards a lusty pull on the reins to prevent falling backward off the saddle. It is an easy matter to actually see a poor horse's back give downward at each step, when packing such a load. No

Plate XXIII *Seated in saddle at gallop. Note that seat leaves saddle slightly at second beat of gallop.*

further proof of the disadvantage from this "back of the horse" position need be given.

The knee and hip joints work so as to open and close together; opening on the upward movement, and closing as the rider descends to the saddle. When posting in balance, with the body well forward, no weight settles on the cantle. The pelvic bones barely touch the saddle/for the rider's weight is all received in the heels, on the knees, and on the inside of the thighs. The knees and calves grip a trifle more firmly than usual, although the grip should never be strong enough to fatigue the rider. There ought to be a feeling that the rider's mass, as he rises to the trot, is helping to carry the horse forward at each stride. That is quite a different thing for the horse, from the case where he is pounded on the back and pulled at each step. When the stirrup straps are vertical, the seat in balance, and posting is done correctly, *the rider's heels are pushed downward and slightly to the rear at each step.* If the body is not inclined forward to keep the balance over the knees, the lower legs and heels are very apt to work to the front, and the rider is immediately "behind his horse." The whole spine should be stretched out and made as tall as possible, in order to ride lightly. The knee and hip joints work as springs to permit the weight to settle softly into the saddle. The rider's position, as he rises to the trot, should give him the feeling that he can dive over the horse's head, if he so desires, or stand in his stirrups, remaining in balance, at the top of the rise.

Before describing how to maintain the correct seat at the gallop, the fact that there are two ways to ride at this gait should be pointed out. In one case, *the rider is fully seated in the saddle,* the weight of the body being distributed from the forward portions of the pelvic bones to the knees. This full seat is normally taken while at a canter or slow gallop, *and also when approaching an obstacle.* It is impossible to know exactly when a horse is going to take off at his jump unless fully seated. Feeling what the horse is going to do, comes through the seat, and permits the experienced rider to anticipate and forestall a horse's defenses. In addition, the legs can only be used tactfully and well, in forcing the horse to jump, when the rider is seated in the saddle. When standing in the stirrups, the lower legs move slightly outward and away from the horse's sides, so that the calves are not in position to instantly squeeze and drive him vigorously forward if he attempts to refuse the jump.

When at a fast gallop across country, racing, or trying to get speed from the horse, as in polo or riding to hounds, the seat should be completely out of the saddle, and the rider should be "in his stirrups." In hunting, however, he should always sit down as he approaches an obstacle. The body is inclined just a trifle farther to the front when standing in the stirrups than when seated in the saddle. As previously explained, this is because the base of support is shortened and farther to the front (extending only from the heel to the inner bone of the knee), and the rider's center of gravity must, as a consequence, be placed farther to the front, through leaning forward from the hips, in order to be in balance over his advanced and shortened base of support.

THE GALLOP, FULLY SEATED

Even when fully seated at the gallop, no effort is made to keep the seat glued tight against the saddle. On the contrary, the buttocks and the pelvic bones come slightly out of the saddle at each stride. The small of the back, or loin, is always under muscular control and kept slightly concave, never humped backward. *Almost all of the motion is taken up by the hip joints when sitting down at the gallop.*

In learning, it is best to keep the loin forcibly hollowed-out, so as to "be with the horse," and make the hip joints do all the work of absorbing the jars. Of course, there is a little opening and closing of the relaxed knee joints.

If the rider places one hand under the buttocks while galloping, there should be almost no weight felt on the hand, providing his seat and position are correct. *The weight is borne mainly on the upper, inner parts of the thighs, and a large part slips through the relaxed knee and ankle joints into the heels. At the gallop, and at the posting trot as well, there should be a feeling of pushing the* l

Plate XXIV *Seated fully at gallop. Shortened stirrups. Approaching jump. Last beat of gallop as horse rolls over right foreleg, prior to period of suspension. Note position of rider's heels and legs; feet braced against stirrups to prevent deranging of seat while legs gently urge horse ahead. Contact with mouth continuous but very light, due to relaxed fingers, elbows, and shoulders.*

buttocks well to the rear toward the cantle, so that the crotch may be in the center, or throat of the saddle. This is only accomplished by hollowing out the smal of the back. If the buttocks are not kept forced to the rear, there will be a strong tendency to let them slip far forward in the saddle. When this occurs, the spine becomes humped, the lower legs slip to the rear, and the knees (providing they are relaxed) and the heels come up, all of which result in weakening and destroying the seat. *When the loin is humped and the knees are stiffened,* with the feet thrust to the front, we have that ridiculous relic, "the old hunting seat."

It is most important that *the heels remain forced far down, and the knees remain almost completely relaxed, so that the calves of the legs may constantly rest against the horse.* The knees are not entirely limp, however, as that would permit the lower legs to slip backward out of position. There is a soft but alert relaxation of the knee joints, so that they are prepared to tighten when necessary. There should be the feeling and the knowledge that if the horse should check his gait suddenly, the brace of the feet against the stirrup treads (because of the low heels), combined with the balance and muscular control of the body (due to hollowing out the small of the back and forcing the buttocks to the rear), would easily prevent your being, thrown forward

Plate XXV. *Last beat of gallop stride, as horse "vaults" over left foreleg. Rider's position faulty. Due to convicted back and loin, and due to not gripping with knees and calves, whole seat slips forward toward pommel. If horse checks suddenly, rider topples forward. Compare with Plate XIV.*

over the horse's neck, despite your forward position. This is a point that the dubious and uninitiated do not understand about the correct forward seat. To be sure, *if the heels are higher than the toes,* and the horse "pecks" (checks suddenly), the lower legs will slip far to the rear and upward, and the rider's mass will roll forward, pivoting over the knees. A fall is always imminent when riding in this manner. Thus, two very important factors in keeping a strong, well-balanced seat at the gallop, whether seated or riding in the stirrups, are: First, *keeping the heels thrust far down, with stirrup straps vertical;* Second, *keeping the buttocks to the rear, so that the loin is hollowed out, the fork deep in the saddle, and the back under muscular control.*

As advocated heretofore, the chest, head and eyes should be kept raised to facilitate keeping the whole body in the correct position. *Here again, if the rider cannot at any moment stand up in the stirrups in balance, without first changing position, he has not sufficient forward inclination from his hips.*

Riding in the Stirrups

This position was partly described earlier in the chapter. At a very fast gallop it is far easier for mount and man. No horse, for instance, could possibly win a race against others in his own class, if the jockey sat down in the saddle. The seat should be close to the saddle, and the weight on the lower thighs, inside of the knees, and in the heels. Here again, keep the back well hollowed-out, the body sharply inclined forward, the chest lifted and the buttocks pushed to the rear. The position is the same as that assumed just before coming into the saddle at the posting trot. The hip joints become immovable at the fast gallop. The rider is actually standing in the stirrups. The knees and calves aid in keeping balance by gripping the saddle and the horse more strongly than when sitting down. The trunk and back are held stiffly, — almost rigid, in fact. The only play in maintaining the balance is in the knee joints. The rider is exactly balanced over his knees, and the horse runs beneath his seat and trunk, which feel no reactions, being completely off the saddle. Except for the work of the knee joints, only the arms move as the elbows open and close to follow with the hands the movements of the horse's neck and head.

For fast galloping and for cross-country work, the stirrups are usually shortened from one to three inches, as this makes it easier to stay in balance with the seat out of the saddle. As previously explained, the shorter the stirrups become, the more the body must be inclined forward, always keeping the small of the back hollowed-out. The jockey's trunk becomes horizontal, due to his very short stirrups. As the shorter stirrups put the buttocks farther to the rear, the trunk must be bent farther forward to keep the mass of the chest, arms and head balanced against the hips, buttocks and lower part of the trunk, over the knees as a center of support. Remember that the knees must not move far to the front when the stirrups are shortened. They are pushed higher on the saddle, and the buttocks farther to the rear, *with the stirrup-straps vertical.*

Do not maintain balance by bracing, or "fixing," the hands on the horse's neck, for the play of his head and neck is very great at a fast gallop, and the hands should follow all these movements. In other words, the seat must be secure without pulling on the reins, or resting the hands on the neck as a support.

When riding in the stirrups at a fast gallop, the upper thighs and crotch are very close to the saddle, often touching it very, very lightly, but never sitting in it or bumping it heavily.

In conclusion, *it is well to remember that when sitting down at the gallop, the reactions on the rider are absorbed by the hip joints, and the whole trunk is pliable and graceful. When standing in the stirrups, the reactions are absorbed by the knee joints, and the trunk is held very stiffly.* The loin, hip and other joints are much stiffer when standing in the stirrups, than when fully seated at the canter or moderate gallop.

Plate XXVI *Riding in stirrups. Seat continuously out of saddle. Hip joints almost rigidly fixed. Compare with Plate XXIII. Both pictures taken at second beat of gallop.*

Plate XXVII *Riding in stirrups. Horse's four feet in air, period of suspension of gallop stride. Note position of horse's head compared with that in Plate XXVI. Oscillation at each stride plainly shown.*

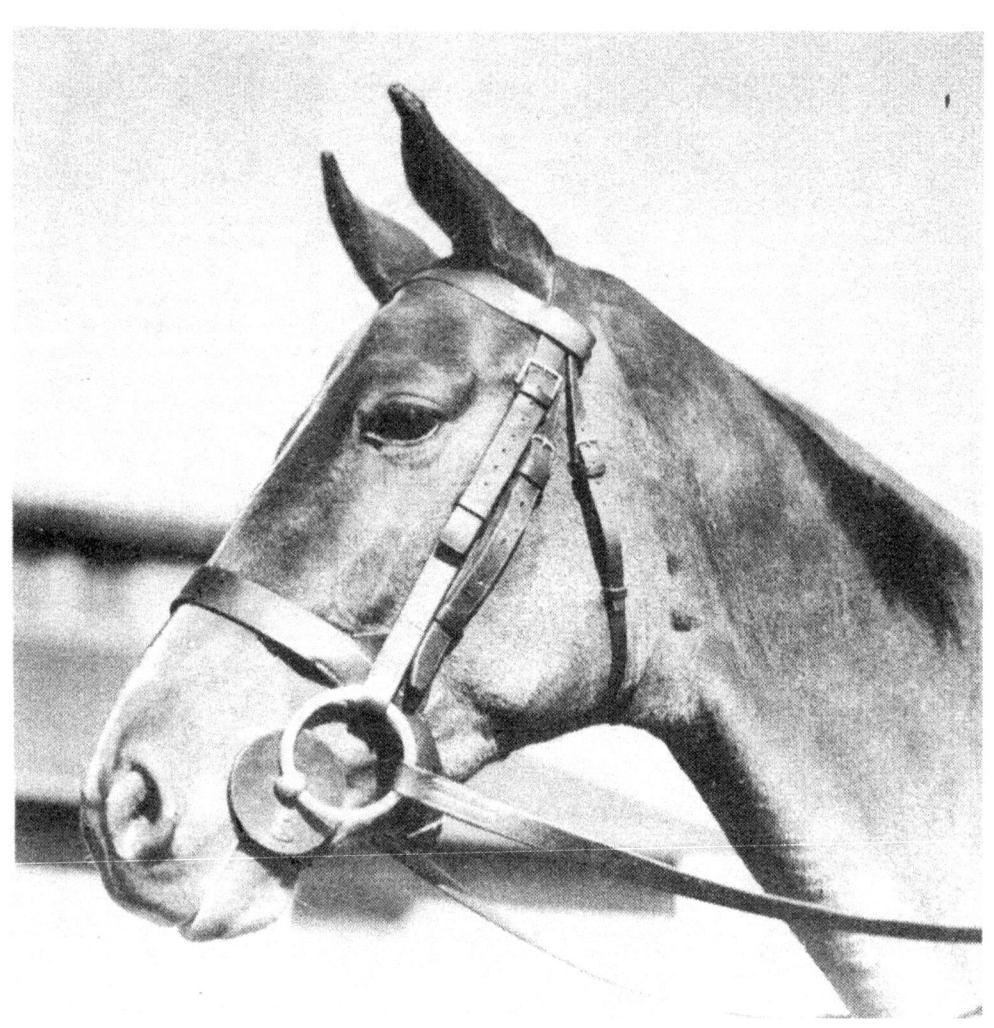

Plate XXVIII

CHAPTER III

THE HORSE'S PERSONALITY

Every rider, novice or veteran, should study the horse's mentality, and the few exceedingly simple psychological principles serving to establish a language between mount and man. The novice, before actually mounting, will do well to spend an hour or two learning something of his horse's personality, while the rider of experience will find that exact theoretical knowledge of the principles involved will greatly improve, expedite, and facilitate training. The world's horsemen are grateful to the distinguished French savant, Gustave le Bon,[17] for the first clearly written truths concerning the psychology of the horse, and for the rules for their employment in riding and training. Prior to his studies, all great horsemen had undoubtedly, either instinctively or as the result of experience, used many of the principles, but none had reduced them to writing. His conclusions will be given, along with other pertinent facts concerning the horse, all of which are easily understood, and should be constantly borne in mind.

First, consider the horse's mind and character. His memory, to all practical purposes, is infallible. Anything unusual he apparently never forgets. This means that if he once gains his will and gets the better of his rider, as, for example, by whirling and returning to the stable, — someday he will certainly try the same trick again. If frightened at a certain point in the road during a promenade, it is a sure bet that he will shy at the same spot a month or more later, even though he may not have passed it in the interim. Countless examples showing the remarkable memory of horses can be given. The important point is to *remember that the horse will not forget.* Therefore, assuming that your mount is well-trained, if he goes contrary to your wishes, you must, then and there, by using tact and persistence compel obedience, and show him, once and for all, that you are the master. On the

---

[17] Gustave le Bon. *L'Equitation Actuelle et Ses Principes:* (Ernest Flammarion, Editor, 26 Rue Racine, 26, Paris.)

other hand, as rapidly as a young or green horse is capable of understanding your desires, he too must be taught that your will is insurmountable.

Horses, just as individuals, differ in character and disposition. Some are bold, but for the most part, they are inclined to be timid. When a horse is truly frightened, unless he is perfectly trained, and so can be forcibly controlled, great patience, calmness, and gentleness must be exercised to restore his confidence. If treated intelligently, after a short time most horses will become fearless of unusual sights. All differ in degrees of nervousness and excitability, but rational training greatly calms the more highly strung types, and increases the courage of the timid ones.

Horses are born mimics. Consequently, one with a vicious trait should not be given a stall near others in the stable, as they will inevitably mimic and acquire the habit. They quickly imitate vices of their neighbors, such as cribbing, kicking, biting, and shying. However, this tendency to imitate is useful in training. Colts can be led beside calm, well-trained, sweet-dispositioned horses, whose good habits they will be prone to copy. Later, to encourage a young horse, while training him to jump, descend steep declines, or cross streams, it aids greatly to let him follow a quiet old hunter.

After a young horse has made considerable progress in his training, he develops the characteristic of trying to understand any new demand made of him by his rider. In other words, he is sufficiently intelligent to become attentive. Hence, riders must constantly use both physical and mental tact to make their wishes clear and unmistakable, and to avoid confusing their horses by the improper, unnecessary, and unintelligible use of reins or spurs. The language of the rider's reins, legs, weight, voice and whip, is called "the aids" in technical equestrian parlance.

It is strange, but perfectly true, that many intelligent people, when riding, fail to use their brains at all. Horses are not mechanical, like automobiles. No two can be controlled exactly alike, which, after all, contributes greatly to the charm of riding. A good horseman must keep his mind constantly active if he is to convey clearly all his desires, and meanwhile learn the idiosyncrasies of the particular mount he is riding. Successful riding does not demand great mental brilliance, but common sense and attention to the work at hand are absolutely essential. It is astonishing that the patient, much-abused livery and riding hall horses ever comprehend the meaning of the brutal, unintelligent actions employed by some of their thoughtless riders.

If punished unjustly, or for some reason not understood, horses develop resentment, restlessness, and vices such as kicking, biting, shying, or running away. The restlessness makes them disagreeable to ride, since, as a result, they habitually fret and jig.[18] Usually, when rightfully punished, they are not resentful, — having, it would seem, as Dr. le Bon states, "a sense of equity."

The horse's intelligence is in general of a rather low order. If badly frightened, he becomes utterly frantic and loses all sense of self-preservation. Fillis[19] claimed that horses have no affection for their masters. However, they do appreciate kind treatment, and resent that which is unnecessarily cruel or unjust. They form warm friendships for other horses (regardless of sex), as well as for other animals. Often a cat or dog will sleep in the stall with a horse, and the latter will exercise the greatest care not to step or lie on his friend. Also, they have a certain cunning. Very often old cavalry horses take great delight in bucking off recruits, whereas when old soldiers mount them, they immediately appreciate the difference in riders, and behave most admirably. All in all, horses have approximately the intelligence of children two years of age, and a person who loses his temper with them, for what is generally due to his own lack of skill, should either become introspective, or forsake horsemanship.

Our equine friends are, for the most part, patient, faithful servants, giving much in return for little. Those with thoroughbred blood, — and many without, — will usually go until they drop, if called upon, — game to the end. Since they cannot tell of their ills or grievances, a horseman worthy of the name learns to study them with a benevolent, observing eye, and thus discovers all they cannot tell. So each rider should realize the part that his horse plays in their partnership, and in all justice, give his personality and needs the study and humane consideration that his unselfish service so surely merits.

Having glanced at the salient points of the horse's mental equipment, the next important step is to appreciate the simple psychological principles which Dr. le Bon has shown to be fundamental in training and riding. The applicable laws of the "association of ideas" are, First — *"When impressions have been produced simultaneously, or have followed one another instantly, it is sufficient that one be presented to the mind in order that the others also immediately present themselves;"* and Second — *"Present impressions revive past impressions which resemble them."* As a very simple example of the application of the first principle, assume that the rider, during the first mounted lesson of a very green, untrained colt, endeavors to stop him by pulling on the reins. The youngster will have no idea why his mouth is being subjected to the pain and annoyance of the bit, and as a result will try, with every defense that comes to his mind, to escape it. He will throw his head, sometimes increase

---

[18] To mix the gaits, and take uncadenced, irregular stept.

[19] Fillis James Fillis' book *Breaking and Riding*

his gait, and usually only as a last resort, come to a mystified halt. If, at the exact instant that he halts, the rider immediately ceases applying tension to the reins, the colt will begin to associate the idea of halting with that of escaping the pain of the bit. After a few repetitions of the lesson, the slightest tightening of the reins will cause him to halt. So lesson number one will have been learned, and a step toward establishing a mutually comprehensible language will have been accomplished.

From the first law of the "association of ideas," also is derived the old rule, *"Reward should instantly follow obedience; and punishment, disobedience."* Thus, to hasten or to confirm the training, — in the example just described, of teaching a green colt to halt, — a further reward can be given at the instant he stops, by patting him on the neck, an attention which all horses particularly like. Henceforth he will mentally associate the halting with the two rewards, — escaping the bit's annoyance, and the caress on the neck. Always, when a horse grasps for the first time what the rider is trying to teach, rewards should be instantly lavished on him. Ceasing to use reins and legs, pats on the neck, encouraging words, a lump of sugar, and, above all, a few moments' rest from his lesson, furnish the appreciated rewards. They must, however, be given immediately in order to establish the association of impressions. Similarly if defenses or disobediences are presented, punishment of the proper type must at once ensue. Thus, if after the horse has learned that pressure from the rider's legs means "go ahead faster," he is sulky, lazy, or balky, — the spurs should be instantly and energetically applied, until he moves briskly to the front, and at the gait desired. Their action should cease with equal promptness when the horse has obeyed. It is stupidly brutal to punish a horse even so late as a few seconds after he has committed an offense, for at that time he no longer associates it with the punishment. Often a rider is seen punishing his horse for having refused a jump, *after* leaving the show ring. This brutality simply confuses the horse, and inspires in him a fear of all show-ring environment. The horse should have been punished by vigorous use of the spurs, at the spot and exact instant he refused.

Applying the same rule to an animal which kicks at persons who pass him in the stable, — the cure is to anticipate his kicking, and carry a strong whip, with which to give him a memorable blow across the hind legs at the instant he lashes out. Naturally, you must stop short of passing in the rear of a kicker when administering the punishment. One good blow at a time is enough, — to continue the whipping after all idea of kicking has left the horse's mind, will only dissipate the benefit of the lesson. Likewise, if a horse "cowkicks"[20] when the rider uses his spur, — the answer is to use it

---

[20] Cowkicks. Kicking out to the side, with a pawing motion of the hind leg.

Plate XXIX. *"Buddies"*

again vigorously — and immediately — each time he kicks. Ultimately he will discover that kicking brings an instantaneous and highly disagreeable reaction — whereupon the kicking will cease.

Next, an example of the application of the second psychological law previously quoted, — "Present impressions revive past impressions which resemble them," — will be described. A trained horse, mounted and at the halt, when his rider touches him with his right spur, should move his hind quarters[21] over to the left, — that is, give way to the pressure of the right leg, or spur. The simplest way to begin instruction in this lesson is while dismounted. The dismounted rider holds the horse by the bridle reins with his right hand, close up to the bit, while standing near the colt's shoulder. With a riding crop he then taps the colt on his right side, just in rear of the girth, near where the heel will rest when mounted. Generally the instinctive reaction of the colt is to push his haunches toward the molesting whip. The rider continues the taps, gradually increasing their severity, until the colt finally moves his hind quarters around to the left. *Immediately* the tapping is stopped, and the colt caressed and softly encouraged with the voice. In a few short lessons, he will move the croup around smoothly, crossing his right hind leg in front of his left, at the lightest tap of the whip. As a result of this lesson, he will obey the touch of the rider's leg or spur when mounted — a similar impression — usually without hesitancy, if the whip lesson has been well-taught. If he does not, the rider combines taps, — with the whip held in the right hand while holding the reins in the left, — with simultaneous squeezes of his leg, or touches with the spur. When obedience is obtained, the whip is no longer used.

In this manner, all lessons are progressively taught, proceeding from the simple ones to the more complex.

Two things confirm lessons given horses, and, little by little, make obedience to the rider's demands subconscious reflexes. These two are *repetition*, and *the occasional administering of a strong impression*. The latter leaves a more indelible effect, and so saves time. Hence, as indicated before, after your horse knows what you are asking him to do, apply your "aids" sharply to obtain instant obedience, if he displays any reluctance, willfulness, or laziness. Ultimately, obedience becomes automatic, if your signals are precise.

In epitomizing the essentials of riding and training, deducible from the knowledge of the horse's brain and psychology, the following thoughts are repeated:

The horse's mentality is very limited.

His memory is amazingly excellent.

He is naturally timid, and, inclined to imitate the good and bad habits of other horses.

Two predominant characteristics are: resentfulness of unjust punishment, and appreciation of merited kindness.

Due to his child-like mind, training should progress very slowly, one simple step to another.

---

21 Hind quarters. See Plate II, Exterior of the Horse.

Horsemen must use their common sense to avoid confusing the horse by unmeaning uses of the reins or spurs.

Only attempt those things which can surely be enforced, for the horse's cunning lets him perceive the inability of the rider to enforce his will, and he never forgets the trick he used to gain the upper hand.

Punishment and reward must always be given simultaneously with, or instantly after, the disobedience or obedience, respectively, in order to follow the law of "the association of ideas."

Strong use of the "aids," after the horse unquestionably knows your desire, hastens subconscious, reflexive obedience.

Never punish a horse for not obeying a signal he does not understand.

Never punish him by brutal jerking on the reins, as this will ruin his mouth.

Plate XXX *Hands following movements of horse's head and neck. Body inclined forward; elbows relaxed and falling naturally just in front of body; horse at walk.*

Plate XXXI *Normal manner of holding single rein.*

CHAPTER IV

THE AIDS

General Remarks

The rider's hands and legs are the principal agencies used in training and riding the horse. The weight, voice, and whip are additional "aids," but are not nearly so important. Spurs are considered part of the legs.

As indicated in Chapter III, the judicious, intelligent use of the aids during breaking and training, and the careful following of correct psychological principles of training, will gradually teach the horse to understand the well-defined language of the aids, by which the rider may conduct and control him. The more perfectly he is trained and ridden, the more nearly telegraphic in its speed this means of communication becomes. As mutual understanding is perfected, the aids become more and more delicate, and the horse's responses are more quickly and lightly executed. This accord and confidence between horse and rider provide no end of thrill and satisfaction to a true horseman. Crude, visible movements of the rider's hands and legs disappear, and the application of the aids is imperceptible to any save the skilled observer, while the horse apparently executes all commands contentedly and of his own free will. As a great French rider once said, the perfectly trained horse "obeys the wind from the rider's boot."

Hands

The use of the hands through the medium of the reins and bits is the most important means of control. Also, finesse of hands is the most difficult part of horsemanship to master. However, after the average rider has a secure, well-balanced seat, — and not *before*, — he can acquire, *through thoughtful practice,* great skill with his hands, and to an amazing degree

Plate XXXII *Normal position of hands. Correct seat with normal length stirrup straps. Length suitable for hacking and training.*

develop their technique. In high-school[22] riding, the fingers must work with the precision and delicacy of a violinist's. Horsemen are prone to forget that the technique of hands is always subject to improvement, and that at no definite time are they ever completely "educated" or "made." Progress in their skill is limitless. Remember that always the psychological principles involved in horse training govern the actions and use of the hands. They resist disobedience and concede to obedience, and the concession must be coincident with the obedience.

The astonishing lack of educated hands is largely the result of failure to "use the head." Constant thought while riding, particularly during a colt's training, must be given to the hands, until finally their precise, tactful use, and the horse's prompt response become mutual reflexes. The hands' actions must always convey the rider's wishes in *exactly the same manner*, so that the horse never may be confused as to what is desired.

Successful schooling and training demand intense concentration; the mind must work even more continuously than does the body. Since the horse's mentality is low, long lessons greatly fatigue his power of attention, and are liable to produce irritability. *Hence, an important principle of training is to give the colt short lessons with frequent periods of rest.*

---

[22] High-school riding. See note on page 4, *"haute école."*

The "Normal Feel"

In order that the rider may be in continuous communication with his horse, and that the effects produced by the bit may softly and instantly convey to him the rider's will, the reins must first be correctly adjusted in length, so that they are gently stretched and taut. Correct adjustment of the reins should allow the rider sufficient play with his elbows, wrists, and hands, to manipulate them easily. The "feel" produced on the mouth by the taut reins is not heavy. At the walk, trot, and canter, the "normal feel" is equal to a force of approximately one pound's intensity. This soft, steady contact with the mouth is maintained by having the elbows partly bent, and the joints of the shoulders, wrists, and fingers almost completely relaxed. They remain relaxed as long as the horse goes at the gait and rate, and in the direction desired. Hands, softly relaxed in this manner, are called "passive."

Position and Function of the Elbows

Normally the reins will be correctly adjusted when the rein and forearm form a straight line to the bit. (See Plates XXIV, XXVI, and XXVII.) If the reins are too long, there will be an angle formed at the hand, by the rein and forearm, destroying the desirable straight line. *Contact of unvarying intensity is principally maintained by the flexibility and play of the elbow joints, which smoothly open and close in order to follow the oscillations of the horse's head and neck.* These oscillations are large at the walk and gallop; almost imperceptible at the trot. Therefore, in following them at the walk or gallop, the hands must move forward and backward; *they should not, however, bob up and down* as a result of the reactions of the horse's gait on the rider's body. The elbow joints must compensate for the body's up and down movements, as well as for the oscillations of the horse's head and neck. The hands are normally about four to ten inches in advance of the pommel arch of the saddle, and from two to six inches higher than the horse's withers. As the body is inclined farther to the front at the posting trot and gallop, a shorter hold is taken on the reins than when at the walk or canter. By so doing, the straight line from elbow to bit is maintained, which gives the smoothest, most efficient action of the hands. *The elbows, due to the forward inclination, hang a little in advance of the body.* They should never be to the rear of it, as the reins would then be too long for the hands to act efficiently or smoothly on the bit. *The upper arms fall naturally and remain relaxed, except when applying increased tension on the reins.*

The play of the elbow joints, and the prevention of the hands bobbing up and down, may be practiced by placing the tips of the little fingers lightly on the horse's neck, just in front of the withers, and holding them there with the reins barely stretched, while at the posting trot. The elbows must then

Plate XXXIII *Reins a trifle too long. Line from elbow to bit not straight; elbow too far to rear. Seat excellent. Horse at canter.*

Plate XXXIV *Reins correctly adjusted in length. Elbows have room for much play. Compare with Plate XXXIII.*

of necessity open and close, in order to keep the little fingers in place on the neck as the body moves up and down. This exercise cannot be executed at the walk or gallop, as the horse's head moves forward and backward at these gaits, and the hands, as stated, should follow the movements.

How the Reins Are Held

With a single rein, such as generally is used with a snaffle bit alone, (See Chapter V), the reins enter the two hands between the little and third fingers, passing up through the palms, and out over the index fingers. The thumbs are placed on top of the reins, pressing them against the middle joints of the index fingers, which prevents the reins from slipping.

When both reins are held in one hand, the rein from the empty hand enters between the ring and middle fingers, or between the middle and index fingers, as desired. The two bights, (loose ends of the reins), then pass over the index finger, and are held in place by the thumb, as is the case when the reins are held in the two hands.

If the reins are held in both hands, when using a double bridle, (one having both the curb and snaffle bits, often called "bit and bridoon"), or with a Pelham bit, (See Chapter V), the snaffle rein enters each hand underneath the little finger, and the curb rein enters between the little and ring fingers. The two reins run up together through the palm and out over the index finger, and are held in place by the thumb.

If all reins are held in one hand, one curb rein enters between the little finger and the ring finger, the other between the ring and middle fingers; one snaffle underneath the little finger, the other between the middle and index fingers. The bights pass out of the palm over the index finger, and are held down by the thumb. Thus the snaffle reins are always outside the curb reins, relative to the horse's neck and to the fingers.

There are numerous ways of holding the reins, many of which may be satisfactory. However, those just given are thought to be as good as, if not better than, any of the others.

Normal Position of the Hands

When the reins are held correctly, the backs of the hands are at an angle of about forty-five degrees with the horizontal, in a natural, easy position. Many riders have tense, stiff arms, elbows, and hands, oftentimes because their hands are held awkwardly. The upper arms, as stated, fall naturally, and remain relaxed; the elbows are always partly bent; the hands hold the reins with partially relaxed fingers, except when they become active to indicate some movement to the horse with the reins. The prolongation of forearms and reins has been discussed, and if this rule is followed, the reins are almost automatically held at the correct length.

The backs of the hands ought not to be turned up horizontally, as this throws the elbows out in a stiff, ugly attitude; nor, on the other hand, should they be held downward or perfectly perpendicular. Both positions, being unnatural, are therefore stiff. Many of our military riders have been incorrectly taught this method of holding the backs of the hands perpendicularly. The idea behind that faulty teaching was to overcome the awkward habit just mentioned, of carrying the backs up and the elbows out. To correct that habit, a beginner may be required to keep the backs of the hands perpendicular until such time as he learns to let the elbows fall naturally, near, and just in front of the body. With the backs of the hands up and the elbows out, the rider stiffens and raises his shoulders, since the elbows can only be held outward by contracting certain shoulder muscles. Any habitual contraction of arm or shoulder muscles makes poor hands.

When the rider learns to carry his hands easily and gracefully, the backs should be, as stated, at about forty-five degrees with the horizontal. Also, *the backs of the hands should be in prolongation of the forearms; there should be no angle formed between hand and forearm, by bending the wrists.* Forearms, wrists, and fingers work in a straight line when the hands are passive. Exceptions to this rule will be noted in describing various actions of the hands and wrists.

So, in taking the reins, reach for them in an easy manner, just as though accepting a proffered cigarette, — no stiffness or death-like clutch is needed.

Length of Reins

If the reins are held with the hands too close to the body, they are generally too long, and the hands' actions are abrupt, due to the large gestures necessary to produce an effect on the mouth. These clumsy effects are not clear to the horse. Moreover, with the reins too long, the rider is forced to use the heavy muscles of the shoulder joints if he attempts to check his, horse, since the elbows are too far to the rear and too much bent to produce any action through further flexion. Using the shoulder joints is unnecessarily clumsy and is brutal to the horse's mouth. With the reins exceedingly long, the hands can exert no immediate action whatever; hence the horse, if frightened, can escape control and bolt, before the reins can be shortened.

When the reins are held too shortly, the elbow joints are straightened, which causes stiff arms and rough, jerky hands, since none of the requisite play at the elbow joints remains. It should be remembered that when the body's inclination is increased for any reason, in order to have the same bend at the elbows, and to have the forearms and reins form straight lines, the reins must be shortened. In jumping, it is essential to have the reins short enough to guard control of the horse without having to lean backward or change position in the saddle, while approaching the jump.

A horse should, of course, be trained to go well with a loose rein, but during much of his work, as, for instance, in riding fast after hounds, where he may be required to execute changes of speed and direction promptly, the reins should be stretched so that communication and control are continuous. During training, a colt should be taught to accept and search for the constant, gentle support on the bit, without raising or lowering his head to an unnatural or ungraceful position. This vital matter of a correct head carriage will be discussed later.

"Good Hands"

When the rider can keep a softly stretched rein of unvarying intensity, with hands that are gentle and elastic, he may be said to have "good hands." However, through lack of technique, he may not, as yet, have developed "educated hands."

There are other points which a possessor of good hands must know and practice. He must realize, for example, that the normal feel on the stretched rein increases in strength as the speed at any gait increases. At the extended trot and fast gallop, the feel on the mouth is quite frank. *However, this feel is never an effect of pulling on the reins.* It is a contact and support that the horse learns to reach for, and by which a rider with good hands maintains communication with his mount without jerking his mouth. A horse that seeks such contact is often said to "take a nice feel on the bit." There should be a sense of "feeding the reins out" to give the horse freedom of movement, without abandoning control.

A rider who is "back of his horse" at the trot or gallop, through not having sufficient forward inclination of his trunk to be in balance, will seldom have good hands, since he habitually pulls on the reins to keep himself in the saddle, especially when his horse unexpectedly increases his gait. Thus he fails to give proper freedom of movement to the head and neck, and as a result, the horse becomes a puller. There are, no doubt, some excellent riders who can take any position in the saddle and not make a horse pull. These are rare, however, and the mechanical disadvantage to the horse, resulting from a poor seat, remains.

At the gallop, much attention must be paid to following with the hands, the forward and backward movements of the horse's head and neck, made at each stride. If this is not done, *due to stiff and inelastic elbows*, something must give to the hands' resistance. Unless the horse runs away, it usually results in his neck becoming too much arched, (over-flexed), and as a result, the horse, if high-strung, becomes a puller; if phlegmatic, he refuses contact with the hand. One that is hesitant about going forward, and will not accept the normal feel of the bit with his neck extended in a natural manner, but which, on the contrary, hangs back with an over-flexed neck, is "behind his bit." He may sometimes be "behind the bit" as a result of never having been trained as a colt, to accept the normal feel; more often, the condition exists as a result of heavy hands, sharp bits, or both. In any event, there is little control over, or pleasure in riding such types; they have no impulsion or lightness, and consequently lack boldness and freedom of action. An over-flexed horse, since his head is so placed that he never sees "bad going" or a fence until on top of it, is dangerous in the hunting field.

With good hands, the play of the shoulders and elbows not only compensates for the movements of the horse's head and neck, but also for those of the rider's body, relative to the horse's mouth, and so eliminates any unintentional or unnecessary action on the bit. To an observer good hands, despite the compensating movements of shoulders and elbows, appear quiet.

Hands: Active, Passive, Fixed. Educated

When the horse is going in the direction and at the gait and rate desired, the hands are "passive," and "give" and "take," as the expression goes, so as to follow the horse's mouth with the same even tension of rein. Remaining "passive" under these circumstances, as just indicated, is the principal characteristic of "good hands."

However, when the horse is disobedient, or when an effect is produced on his mouth to demand a decrease of gait, change of direction, or some particular movement, *"educated" hands do not "give" but resist, as long as the horse "takes." They only "give" when the horse "gives" and ceases to "take."* These distinctions between "good" and "educated" hands are well brought out by James Fillis in his excellent book called *Principles of Dressage and Equitation a.k.a. Breaking and Riding* [Xenophon Press].

When any effect is produced on the horse's mouth by increased tension on the rein, the rider's hand is said to be "active," in contradistinction to its normal semi-relaxed "passive" condition.

The majority of horsemen make unnecessarily crude, large, and often ineffective gestures in using the hands. When the hand becomes active for any purpose, it is first moved *just the distance necessary to a position where it can best act to produce the result desired on the horse's movement. Then, assuming that the reins are properly stretched and adjusted in length, the half-relaxed fingers close and tighten on them. Finally, the hand is "fixed" in place, maintaining the additional resistance thus produced against the mouth with the bit. This increased resistance continues until the horse obeys the hand, whereupon the fingers instantly relax as a reward for his obedience.* Oftentimes they may close again almost instantly, if the horse has not completed the movement desired, or in case the opposition he has presented has not been entirely subdued. Fixing the hand often requires a simultaneous fixing, or immobilizing, of the elbow and shoulder joints, where the horse's resistance is strong and stubborn. In other words, the whole arm is "set." In this case, the whole arm also relaxes simultaneously with the fingers, in rewarding the horse.

The above method of using the hands is very simple, after some practice, and is much more efficacious than pulling with the weight of the body and strength of the arms. It must be remembered that, as was mentioned in describing the seat, *the knees must grip the saddle, the lowered heels be braced against the stirrups, and the back muscles tightened by thrusting the buttocks somewhat to the rear, when setting up a strong resistance with the fixed hands, in order to compel a horse to obey.* Such powerful action will normally only be necessary against unruly mounts, when strong opposition to the effects of the hands might pull the rider out of position and weaken his seat.

In pulling, instead of resisting by fixing the hand, the rider usually does not detect the horse's concession. As a result, his hand, instead of relaxing, flies to the rear when the horse gives. No reward follows the horse's giving; consequently, with pulling hands, the mouth is never improved. A man who pulls, instead of resisting with fixed hands, may be likened to one who is pulling on a rope against an opponent in "tug of war." If the opponent unexpectedly lets go his end of the rope, the puller falls backward. If, however, the latter has prepared for such a contingency, by remaining in balance and using his muscles, rather than his weight, in resisting his opponent, he will not be surprised, and fall backward. *This should be the thought in using the reins; to maintain a balanced seat and resist, rather than pull.* The fixing of the hands need not be absolutely rigid and immovable in all cases. Tact must be used; the finger, elbow, and shoulder joints set up a resistance more or less fixed, depending on the type of horse, and his degree of training. If the lightly-fixed hands are pulled slightly out of their position by a young, partly-trained horse, they are promptly replaced and fixed a little more firmly.

The more highly educated the hands become, the more quickly and smoothly they resist or relax at the appropriate time, and the more accurately they measure the correct amount of resistance. *In many cases where the hand has been carried to the rear and fixed, it is necessary to relax the whole arm and move the hand forward in addition to relaxing the fingers, in order to cede entirely to the horse's obedience.* For instance, when stopping quickly from great speed, as in polo; the hand is first moved to the rear (as the pony's head comes to the rear during the oscillation it makes at each gallop stride), to a point where it can exert the resistance required to stop the pony; the fingers are smoothly and tightly closed on the reins, and the hand is fixed in position. The trained pony's jaw and poll "give" and flex to this resistance, while his neck and head are somewhat raised. Just as he is relaxing his jaw and poll in stopping, the fingers must also relax, and *the hand must move forward* to give him his head completely as he halts. The aim always should be to let the horse put his head in a natural, comfortable position as soon as he has ceased resisting, the hands moving to whatever position permits this.

Where the horse does not at once obey the action of the hand, it continues to *"resist"* by remaining fixed. It steadily maintains the increased tension on the taut rein at exactly the same intensity, until the horse yields. A series of pulls and givings never teach a horse anything. Often with the fixed hand, the fingers may "work the bit" a trifle to break up tactfully the resistance of the horse's jaw, as will be discussed under "Vibrations." *The intensity of the hand's resistance must be just equal to that offered by the horse; never more.*

The ability to fix the hand in the necessary place, with a resistance exactly equal to the horse's resistance, and to yield the exact instant the horse yields, is the whole secret of "educated hands." Without this ability, the true art of riding, and the feeling given by a perfect mouth, are unknown.

Both hands, or one at a time, may resist, depending on what is desired. The hand that is not active is normally soft and passive, giving what rein is necessary to allow the active hand to place the horse's head in the position suitable for executing the called-for movement. Take, for example, a turn to the right by direct tension to the rear on the right rein: as the horse turns his head to the right, due to the resistance on the right rein, the left hand moves to the front slightly, in order to let the head turn. This passiveness prevents the left hand's contradicting the right.

A hand, as will be described under "Rein Effects, " may have to move to the left and up; to the right and rear; to the right and forward, etc., so as to act in the correct direction against the bit in securing a certain movement from the horse. *Only after it is correctly placed, do the fingers close on the stretched rein to augment the tension.* Let it be repeated that *only the resistance necessary to make the horse obey, — no more; no less, — is used by the skillful rider.* This may equal only a few ounces on an obedient, well-trained horse, while on a spoiled rogue, a hundred pounds maybe required. No matter how obstinate the horse maybe, the instantaneous yielding to his obedience, whenever it comes, provides the only way of improving his mouth and manners.

"Educated hands" can be acquired by any moderately good horseman, but not in a day or a week, and *only through thinking when in the saddle, and reflecting on results obtained, after a ride.* Such hands can quickly make a perfectly trained horse out of a green colt, and ultimately reclaim most

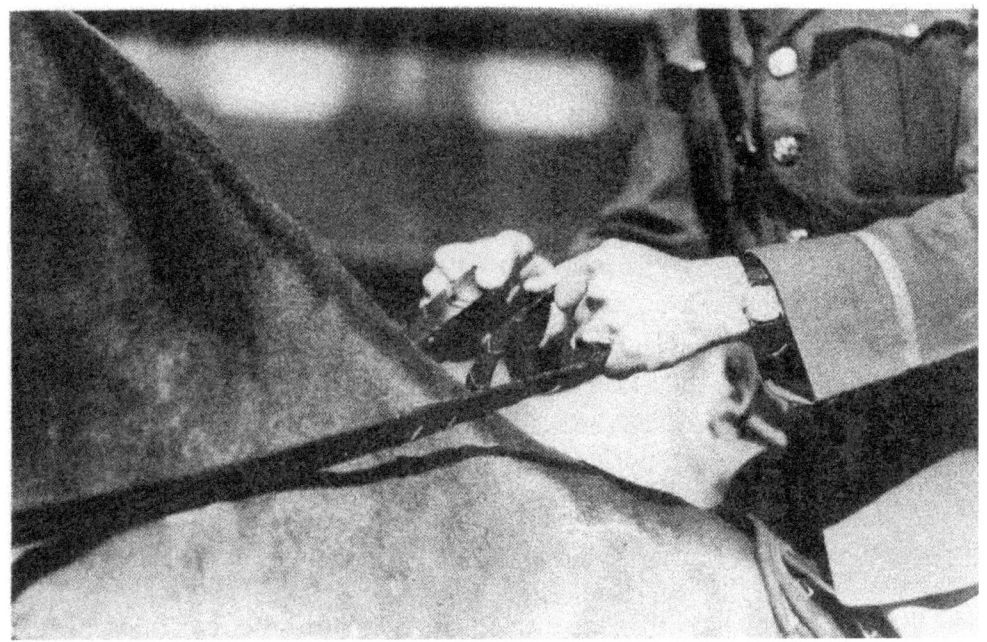

Plate XXXV *Hands "fixed;" reins stretched; fingers tightly closed; arms and elbows set. When horse "gives," hands and arms relax and "give."*

bad-tempered and spoiled horses. The only necessary adjunct to assist educated hands are the legs, which will be dealt with later.

To recapitulate; the keynote of educated hands is "resistance," not "pulling." To establish only the resistance equal to the force with which the horse is opposing the rider's will, requires a "fixed" hand. The "fixed" hand is placed in the appropriate position to obtain a certain reaction from the horse. There, with just the proper resistance, it remains still, relative to the horse's mouth, and undisturbed by the movements which he makes with his head, neck, or mouth, in order to escape the bit's action. As frequently emphasized, the hand can only be fixed when the rider has a secure, steady seat, and independence of the aids.

In extreme cases, it may be necessary to fix the hands on the saddle pommel, or on the horse's neck, to overcome an obstinate or spoiled horse. With such a horse, when the hands are thus fixed, *the heels of the thumbs should be placed against the saddle or neck, so that the fingers may feel when the horse yields,* and instantly relax to reward him. It is also helpful to clamp the elbows or wrists against the body when first learning to fix the hands. This can be done easily at the walk or slow trot. While the reins are usually a little too long with the hands in this position, it permits the rider to get the "feel" of the "fixed" hand.

Educating the Horse to "Educated Hands"

In schooling a young horse, or one which has not been accustomed to being controlled by educated hands, *some small yielding or softening of the fingers should instantly recompense the slightest concession he makes.* Let us again take the example of the rider turning his horse to the right by direct tension on the right rein. The first step is to carry the right hand, (active), slightly outward to the right and backward; secondly, with the rein adjusted and stretched, the fingers are gradually closed, progressively setting up a resistance against the horse's jaw; thirdly, the hand is fixed in place. On a relaxed and obedient horse, the effect is to turn his nose, head, and neck slightly to the right. This increases the weight supported by the right foreleg, and disturbs the horse's equilibrium in that direction. As a result, he moves off on a large curve to the right.

However, a green colt may resist the hand's action, by stiffening the neck and holding the head straight to the front. The rider must increase the tension slightly, by moving the hand a little farther to the rear, and fixing it adamantly in place. The passive left hand always gives to the front the exact amount the active right hand is drawn to the rear. It may be some moments before a stubborn horse or a green colt decides that resistance to the fixed hand is futile, but after trying various defenses, as an escape from the bit's annoyance, he will finally turn his head and neck to the right. While obedience is not yet complete, the instant he yields the least trifle, there should be a momentary softening of the fingers of the right hand. They are then again closed before he has time to carry his head back to the front, and the hand's action demands a further obedience.

In other cases, after bending the neck readily to the right, the colt may continue moving to the front in his original direction. Here the hand must be drawn a trifle farther to the rear and again fixed, until, in addition to turning the neck and head, he commences his turn to the right, which must also be promptly rewarded. A pat on the neck with the left hand, coincidental with the rein reward, is helpful, as a horse is singularly appreciative of that caress, and will thereafter associate this pleasant sensation with obedience to the right rein. If he bends his neck too far, its bending is limited by the left hand's being fixed low down by the left shoulder.

In all cases, after the colt starts his turn to the right, the rider's fingers relax, but immediately tighten again, gently continuing these alternate effects intermittently, so as to keep the head placed, and sustain the change of direction until the turn is complete. With this movement, as with all others, if rewards are prompt, the colt quickly learns what is desired, and the amount of the hand's resistance gradually may be diminished until the mildest effect suffices to secure the turning of the head and neck and the change of direction desired. The above resistances almost invariably are encountered in all colts. The rider's legs come to the assistance of the hands in all these cases, as will be shown later.

The skill and rapidity with which reward follows obedience, and resistance meets opposition, will, in a large measure, determine the time necessary to train the colt and make his mouth. It will be discovered that it is the rider's legs, more often than the hands, that mete out punishment.

Jerking the Mouth

The application of increased tension on the reins should always be smooth and gradual. *Never should there be any jerking on a loose rein.* A trained horse ought never to fear the bit, but rather, recognize its painful, irresistible force in case he disobeys. Jerking not only makes him afraid of his bit, but also of the man on his back; both defeat the purposes of rational training, setting it back anywhere from an hour to weeks.

Even when a horse is badly spoiled, obstinate, or violent, the resistance, when fixing the hand against the bits, should be applied *progressively*, until its force is equal to the pull or opposition that the horse is exerting. However, when the hand is finally fixed on a rebellious horse it must remain immovable, until he obeys. Certainly, in the first instance, one may jerk and pull a horse to a slower speed, a halt, or a sharp turn, more quickly than the same thing can be accomplished by the fixed hand and measured resistance. But after succeeding the first time, *through jerking*, one has only unnerved, frightened, and further ruined the horse. Next time under the same circumstances, full of apprehension, he will be even more violent and difficult, and every horse's final defense, when thoroughly frightened, is to plunge about, seeking an opportunity to run away. On the other hand, if educated hands have used intelligent and persistent tact, to slowly but surely secure a concession from the horse, next time he will be calmer and more quickly obedient, since he will have learned a lesson. He has time to reflect during the steady, unbeatable resistance of the hand; whereas he is thrown into uncomprehending panic by brutality. Assuredly he may need repetitions of certain lessons, (particularly in the case of a spoiled horse), but as he grasps the idea being taught, the strength of the resistance may be increased by fixing the hand on a shorter rein. This administers a *strong impression*, which, psychologically, has a more indelible and lasting effect than many weak ones. When he fully understands and ceases fighting, the aids should diminish in intensity.

Abuse indicates lack of intelligence in the man, rather than in the horse. Punishment, justly measured, and given at the proper instant, is essential to training, but punishment, untimely, unnecessarily brutal or incomprehensible to the horse, accomplishes nothing. It merely ruins his disposition and fills him with unreasoning fear. When well-trained, a horse will not have exciting fear of, but great respect for, his master's will. Punishment administered for an offense as much as five-seconds after its commission, is gross stupidity, for the horse no longer associates it with the offense.

Length of Rein with the Fixed Hand

One of the greatest errors committed in using the fixed hand, is that of having the reins too short when the resistance is set up. Never-ending effort should be made to avoid arching a horse's neck too much. With a young horse, particularly, great care should be taken when the hands are fixed. They should not be drawn an inch farther to the rear than is absolutely necessary to accomplish the desired result. Oftentimes a young horse, through ignorance or high-spirits, or an older horse, through ignorance or obstinacy, will not immediately obey the hand's fixed resistance when applied with fairly long reins. However, if the rider patiently perseveres, the horse will normally obey after a greater or less period of time. If an old horse is very hard-mouthed, it will be necessary to use a Pelham bit, or a double bridle, to compel obedience. In any event, set up your resistance and stick to it, even if, in the first lessons, it is a matter of one, two, or three minutes actual time before the horse yields. If you feel you must shorten the rein, or reins, to make him respond, shorten them only a very small amount at a time, then fix the hand again, until he yields by softening his jaw, turning, slowing, or halting, as the case may be. Above all else, avoid folding his neck and head into a ball against his chest. It is surprising how quickly, with a little patience, a horse can be taught to yield to the bit with long reins, while keeping his neck extended.

Resistances Presented by the Horse to the Bit

In general, the horse has three ways of resisting the bit. They are as follows:

1. By stiffly setting the muscles of the lower jaw.
2. By stiffening certain muscles of the neck, particularly in the upper third, just back of the ears, in the region of the poll.
3. By lowering the head and throwing a preponderance of his weight on the rider's hand.

These three general resistances will be discussed in detail, with the three actions of the hands employed in destroying them.

Plate XXXVI *Producing "vibrations." Closing fingers of right hand while those of left relax, to let bit slip an inch or so through horse's mouth, toward right.*

Plate XXXVII *Right wrist bends inward and upward, so that palm of hand turns toward rider's chest to apply additional tension, when closing fingers does not suffice.*

1. Softening or Flexing the Lower Jaw by Means of "Vibrations"

Any young horse, through ignorance of how to "accept the bit," invariably stiffens the muscles of the lower jaw. The same is true of old horses which have been improperly trained or poorly ridden. It will normally require more time to relax an old one's jaw than that of a colt. "Vibrations" is the name applied to the action of the hand used in decontracting the muscles of a stiff jaw.

When more than normal tension is put on the reins, a well-trained horse, instead of resisting their action by contracting his jaw, relaxes it. His mouth partly opens, and when the rider's fingers yield in answer to this concession, he gently closes his jaw again, and softly chews once or twice on the bit, as though feeling it, to be sure the rider has loosened the rein. This softening or flexion of the jaw should always precede the arching, or "direct flexion" of the neck at the poll, which will be discussed later. It should therefore always be taught the colt before teaching "direct flexion." (See Plates XXXVI and XXXVII.)

"Vibrations" to relax the jaw are executed as follows: the snaffle bit is worked back and forth through the mouth by a soft, sawing action on the reins. This sawing, or vibration, is produced by closing the fingers of the right hand, for example, while the fingers of the left hand simultaneously relax to let the bit slip an inch or so through the horse's mouth, toward the right. Then smoothly, slowly, and without delay, the fingers of the right hand partly relax, while those of the left close and slide the bit back toward the left. The wrists may assist the action of the fingers, by bending inward and upward, so that the palm of the hand turns toward the rider's chest. Vibrations are usually executed with a snaffle bit, and the reins remain lightly stretched, the hands carefully avoiding any abrupt or harsh effect to the mouth. Allowing much slack to exist in the rein creates a jerky, irritating effect, which causes immediate stiffening, rather than decontraction, of the jaw.

With a little patience, this gentle sawing, effected by the fingers on the stretched reins, will cause a horse to relax his lower jaw muscles and open his mouth. It is undesirable to force the mouth wide open; it should open only part way. A rider not accustomed to this work, and whose hands are not trained to feel when the jaw yields, should watch the horse's mouth in order to see when it opens. The opening should be instantly rewarded by ceasing the vibrations, and a momentary decrease in the tension on the reins. The cardinal principle of instantaneous reward for obedience applies. At first, this exercise should be executed while the pupil is at a walk or slow trot. For two reasons it will expedite the softening of the jaw, in many cases, to perform the vibrations while moving on a circle of about ten yards radius: First, it facilitates seeing the horse's mouth, since his head is turned slightly in on the curve over which he is traveling. Secondly, in order to keep the horse on the circle, the action of the rider's inside hand will dominate. Where one hand acts more strongly than the other it favors a quicker response to the vibrations than when the two hands act evenly, as when moving on a straight line. After rewarding the horse for softening the jaw, the exercise should be repeated at short intervals of time. Very soon *it will only be necessary to increase the tension on both reins, without vibrations, to secure a jaw flexion.* No attempt should be made to arch the horse's poll at this time. On the contrary, he should be encouraged to keep his neck and head well to the front and rather low, in a natural, unconstrained position. Later, the jaw flexion should be practiced at the normal trot, and canter. With some horses, results can be obtained more quickly at the slow trot, than at the walk.

As a general rule, the vibrations are executed without any increase over the normal feel in the tension on the reins. However, in the case of older, poorly trained, or stubborn horses, it may be necessary to increase the tension when vibrating the bit, in order to compel a yielding of the jaw. In these cases, the rider's legs may have to urge the horse along, in order to prevent his slowing the gait or halting, as a result of the increased tension on the reins.

If, after a horse has learned to promptly relax his jaw in response to the vibrating rein, it is desired to slow his speed or halt, the vibration should be continued, with a little additional tension applied to the reins. The jaw flexion is taught as a preliminary step to decreasing the gait or halting, and is the second step in producing a good mouth. The first step is teaching the colt to accept the normal feel on the bit, with an extended neck. The decrease in gait should only be demanded after the jaw has relaxed and given to the action of the hand.

Thus, it is seen that vibrations teach a soft, relaxed yielding in obeying the rider's hand. This replaces the horse's natural, instinctive stiffening of the jaw against the bit's action. The yielding eliminates heavy pulling, and the rough action of the bit, which is unavoidable with stiff-jawed horses.

As stated, after having perfected the lesson of relaxing the jaw in answer to vibrations, it will be found that soon the same result is obtained by simply increasing the tension on the reins. Vibrations are a means to an end, and with the trained horse, are only resorted to from time to time, when it is necessary to break up an occasional stubborn or whimsical stiffening of the jaw, to which any horse inevitably will return.

It must always be borne in mind that no horse ever becomes perfectly or "automatically" trained. They are all live individuals, never automatons, and therefore subject to indispositions, physical and temperamental, many of which, unfortunately, remain unrevealed to the most solicitous masters. A true horseman must be tolerant. All horses have their idiosyncrasies and "off-days," when a horseman must return, with patience and sympathetic understanding, to a rehearsal of early lessons, in order to reestablish obedience and control. It is these equine vagaries and the innumerable unexpected incidents which arise, that give to horsemanship its never-ending interest. Much of equestrian tact abides in knowing when to compromise, and when to fight it out. Absolute domination should never be attempted unless general conditions, the horse's previous training, and the rider's good temper augur success. The most difficult part of tact in training is to appreciate the exact instant the horse begins to understand and obey what is wanted, and, at that identical instant, to reward his comprehension, obedience, and good will, even though he has not completely understood or executed what has been asked.

2. Direct Flexion of the Poll by the Fixed Hand

The vast majority of young horses stiffen their necks as Well as their jaws in opposition to the bit. The reason is the same as for stiff jaws; they have not been taught to "accept the bit" and relax the poll and jaw, instead of resisting, when additional tension is put on the reins. Some horses stiffen by poking out their necks, heads, and noses almost horizontally, while others thrust them forward and downward in resisting the hand. Either of these conditions is easily rectified, and is a desirable initial reaction to the bit on the part of a colt. A third type of stiffened poll is found in the "star-gazer," a horse which thrusts his nose, head, and neck upward. This type usually has his neck on "upside down," its outline being convex underneath, and concave on top, approximately the opposite shape to that of a neck properly set on. In a green colt, "star gazing" is not difficult to remedy, but when confirmed in an old horse, it is almost incurable. Generally, "upside-down" necks are found on horses with naturally poor conformation. For the method of correcting "star-gazing," continue reading this chapter.

After succeeding in flexing the jaw, direct flexion of the poll is accomplished by a fixed hand, which has been fully described. "Direct flexion" may be called the third step in developing a good mouth, the first being to teach the horse to take a normal feel on the bit, and the second, to flex his jaw. *It is highly essential to delay direct flexion until the horse has been perfectly trained in the first two steps just mentioned.*

Direct flexion results from fixing the hands, and causing the horse to arch the upper third of the neck, in the general region of the poll. The lower two-thirds, and particularly the portion just in front of the shoulders, should remain firm and stiff. This lower part should never be arched, as that lowers and places the head close to the breast. This, in turn, makes him heavy in front, and poorly balanced.

When a horse executes direct flexion correctly, his mouth first opens part way as the jaw relaxes, and his head then moves backward, partly closing the angle formed at the throat by the neck and lower jaw. After the head is placed as a result of the flexion, the mouth closes at once. It only reopens when more rein tension is applied. The neck bends only at the poll. The face approaches the vertical, but should never remain in rear of the vertical, as this condition invariably results from the neck's being over-flexed, particularly near the shoulders. Over-flexion leads to many vices, such as pulling, nervousness, falling back of the bit, heaviness of the forehand, and shortened gaits.

The important points in teaching direct flexion are:

1. To first flex the jaw.

2. To fix the hands, with as long a rein as possible, to avoid over-flexing the neck. The hands must be fairly high when fixed, because usually the bending of the neck will occur above the reins.

3. To maintain fixed hands, until the horse is forced to nod slightly by flexing the poll, which is instantly and lavishly rewarded by relaxing the hands, and by pats on the neck.

4. To use the legs, squeezing with the calves, or touching with blunt spurs, if necessary, to keep the horse up to his gait and speed. Otherwise, he will undoubtedly slow down or stop, as a result of the increased tension of the fixed hand. Tact is necessary, so that the action of the legs is sufficient to maintain the gait, and so that the resistance of the bit is not so severe, as to over-flex the neck, or provoke rebellious defenses.

5. To repeat lessons, progressing very slowly, until the complete direct flexion, as described above, is obtained. This work usually requires several weeks. It should be done at the walk or slow trot, and later at the faster gaits; never at the halt, with a green colt. The slow trot is probably the best gait, as the forward motion can be easily sustained, whereas at the walk, the horse can readily stop, if he resists the bit.

Collection

Gradually, by using intermittent effects on the reins, executed entirely by smoothly opening and closing the fingers of the fixed hands, and by tactful use of the legs to maintain the gait, the flexion of poll and jaw can be held for some time. The horse is then said to be "collected" and "in hand." (See Plate XXXVIII.) The hands and legs, despite certain authors to the contrary, more and more contradict each other by their effects, as a high state of collection is demanded. In other words, the legs urge the horse forward, while the hands restrain him in order to maintain the flexion, and increase his drive and impulsion by engaging his hind feet well forward under his body.

Part of the impulsion is caught against the bit. This increases flexion, not only of the jaw and poll, but of the hocks and knees. Loftier knee and hock action results, which the hands regulate, and the legs produce. Collection requires practice and tact, in order to teach the horse what is desired, without confusing him by the contradictory demands of the aids. After learning to trot, for example, while highly collected, the horse remains very light, with barely stretched reins. Jaw and poll are soft, and increase their flexion at the slightest demand of the hand. The rider's legs constantly must be ready to act to prevent any dying-out of impulsion from the hind legs. For the most part, a high state of collection is totally unnecessary, and except with the most finished riders, is the proverbial "razor in the hands of a monkey." The almost invariable result of demanding high collection is over-flexion. The horse finally develops a permanently over-arched neck; his gaits become high and short; he loses the faculty of extending his neck and going calmly, when given his head, particularly when at speed or in the company of other horses. As a result, if held in hand in company, he fights and pulls; if given his head, he runs away. *The moral indicated is that direct flexion should be very carefully and sparingly employed.* Its purpose should be to insure a good mouth in checking and turning, always allowing the horse to extend his head and neck with a passive hand, under normal circumstances. It is far better to have a horse with a stiff poll, in the hunting field, which goes quietly about his work, than one which has had too much direct flexion and collection, and as a result, has cultivated a distorted neck and brain, causing him to become frantic and prone to run away under excitement.

Plate XXXVIII *Highly collected high school horse. Flexion at poll is correct; face vertical; lofty action; horse lightly balanced, as shown by relaxed fingers and almost floating reins.*

"Placed" Head

A well-trained horse gradually acquires a permanent, graceful, and very slight flexion at the poll when on a stretched rein, while the remainder of the neck is naturally and fully extended. With this head carriage, he is referred to as having his head "well-placed." It is in a position where the bits may act from an advantageous angle, and the horse can easily see everything in his foreground. Due to the relaxation of his poll, back, and loin muscles, he carries himself lightly, and with a minimum fatigue. (See Plate XXXIII.)

Slowing the Gait and Halting

If the hands remain fixed, after flexing the poll and jaw, and the legs do not urge the horse forward, he will slow the gait or halt, as required. The main purpose of the flexions is to make the horse respond easily and quickly to the hand, when slowing the gait or halting. A horse that flexes properly and checks promptly, if the hands' resistance continues, is often spoken of as "coming back easily" to the rider's hand.

It is a physiological fact that the horse's loin, back, and hocks always remain stiff and contracted as long as the muscles of the poll are rigidly stiffened. In that state it is physically impossible for him to engage his hind legs well up under his mass. As a result, he travels more or less awkwardly, depending on the individual's natural gaits, and appears "sprawled out."

Lightness

Direct flexion is therefore a most valuable lesson, if properly taught, and the placing of the horse's head is vitally important in developing good manners and a good mouth. *The process of developing the flexions and placing the head should extend over a long period of time. It ought never to be hurried, remembering always that the horse should retain the habit of extending his head and neck to their normal, natural positions, whenever the hands are passive.* The periods of time during which the horse is flexed, or collected, should be, in the beginning, very brief, and always followed by work with the head and neck fully extended. Flexions have the purpose of facilitating control, while cultivating in the horse that relaxation which should be possessed by any good athlete. The good athlete's relaxation allows all the muscles, not engaged in the particular action, to remain decontracted. This results in a minimum of work in accomplishing any act, and in the horse produces "lightness."

Plate XXXIX *Position of hands after rotating little fingers up and back toward chest, in excuting "half-halt." Elbows also close when "half-halt" is severe. Tension is next abandoned momentarily.*

3. Correcting a Horse Which Resists with his Weight, by "Half-Halts"

As has been shown, vibrations are used in the case of resistance with a stiff jaw; fixed hands, where the horse stiffens the poll. Now the third general resistance, in which the horse uses his weight, will be briefly discussed. This is generally found in a horse poorly trained originally, or, in one well trained, which has been subsequently ruined by poor hands. The resistance usually occurs from lowering the head, carrying the face back in rear of the vertical, and over-flexing the neck just in front of the shoulders. In this position, the horse deliberately throws the weight of his head, neck, and shoulders onto the rider's hand, and pulls. Sometimes this is done with the purpose of running away, if possible, but more often because he has lost the ability to take the bit, extend his head and neck, and carry himself lightly.

There are innumerable variations in the manner of operation of these spoiled rascals. The only way of permanently remedying any of them, is by complete re-training, and "re-making" their mouths. "Re-making" is always much more difficult than the original "making," but can be effected with certain horses if enough time and great patience are used. The only type which presents enormous difficulties is one which rounds its neck completely over, tucking the head against the breast. This horse has lost all rigidity of the lower portion of the neck, and presents a rather hopeless problem. There is nothing left with which to guide him. On the contrary, any sound horse which resists by stiffly stretching and lowering the neck, can usually be reclaimed in a short time. The over-arched, limp-necked lugger, however, usually has been completely ruined, as far as ever again providing a pleasant ride is concerned. If sluggish, he is back of the bit until excited or tired, when, through having lost the ability to take a normal feel, with a comfortably extended neck, he becomes utterly uncontrollable or a frightful puller. Fortunately, he is unable to run very fast with his head against his breast, since the extension of his legs is automatically curtailed. If given his head when excited, such a horse is completely "at sea," and becomes a floundering run-away.

The "half-halt" is the rein effect most generally used in combatting a horse which throws his weight on the rider's hands. This effect does not provide a sure means of curing a confirmed rogue, or of reclaiming a spoiled mouth. It is merely a method of preventing a horse with a good mouth from learning to lug in the manner described, and of temporarily managing a low-beaded puller.

The half-halt is executed with a stretched rein, which prevents its becoming a jerk. Jerks only further terrify and ruin a difficult horse. With a horse throwing his weight on the hand, there will, of course, be no doubt about the reins being stretched, but they should never be allowed to go entirely slack, just prior to using the half-halt, in order to make the action more severe. The effect is accomplished by a quick, sharp upward and rearward action of the bit.

This is done by rotating the wrists, so that the little fingers move inward, upward, and toward the rear, in the direction of the rider's chest or chin. A quick, strong effect on the bit is produced, which, if need be, the elbows and forearms accentuate, whereupon the hands quickly relinquish all support for a fleeting second and then resume contact without a jerk. The half-halt would be a jerk when executed, if the reins were not stretched. The effect is to force the horse to shift his balance to the rear, off the forelegs and the rider's hands. The bicep muscles actually lift the head of a stubborn horse. (See Plate XXXIX.)

The half-halt may be executed with one or both hands, varying the procedure so as to refuse the horse a fixed support to pull against, and, at the same time, to punish him for his willful resistance to the hands. The half-halt may operate on either the snaffle or curb bit, or both; the snaffle usually being more effective. The amount of force actively applied should be regulated, as usual, by the amount of resistance the horse is presenting. With a colt, trying to lower the head in play, it would be only the lightest of effects, using the force in the fingers alone; with a rogue, the fingers, wrists, forearms, and biceps may be called into action.

General Remarks on Hands

The subject of hands is inexhaustible. Only the three general types of resistance, and the three counteracting rein effects, with a few detailed descriptions to illustrate their application, can be embraced in the scope of this book. There are an infinite number of effects, depending upon the amount and direction of force applied, or upon the particular combination of vibrations, fixed hands, and half-halts, which may, and often must, be used. It is impossible to describe every type of defense and the corresponding rein effects used to defeat it. Moreover, as will be shown, the action of the rider's legs in abetting the hands, can modify each effect. It will be found, in practice, that the use of the hands is not as complicated as the above statements may indicate.

Riding is, after all, an art, and while the principles governing the use of the aids are unchanging, the application of the aids in carrying out these principles is rarely the same in any two particular instances. Experience and practice based on prior theoretical knowledge, can make an excellent rider, who intuitively applies the correct combination of aids called for by the defense. A finished horseman anticipates and uses the necessary aids to prevent any defense the horse may attempt. Practice teaches the rider to feel, by means of his seat and hands, all the unusual movements a horse makes, prior to committing an offense.

Variations in the Positions of the Hands

The normal position of the hands, when the horse is going quietly, in the direction and at the gait desired, has been described as from two to six inches higher than the horse's withers, and from four to ten inches in front of the saddle. The measurements vary somewhat with the rider's size, and the angle at which he is leaning forward. When the hands are used for any purpose, — in other words, become active, — they must be moved to a position where they can best accomplish the desired result. In training, and during trouble, they will oftentimes be in most unorthodox positions compared with those taken on a perfectly trained and well-behaved horse. *There can be no fixed rule.*

Many riders, particularly in the Army, have been wrongly instructed to habitually carry their hands low. As a result, many continue to do this, when, under certain circumstances, the action of low hands is utterly ineffectual, and may even aid the horse in his defenses. Instead of having been taught principles of rein effects, they have been given rules, and in equitation, there are few rules which have no exceptions.

One rule which is unchanging in regard to the action of the rider's hands, but not in regard to their position, is as follows: *Whenever the horse places his head in a position other than the correct one, the hands are moved where they can increase tension on the bit and make his mouth uncomfortable.* In these cases, they must be so placed that the horse cannot possibly escape the bit's tension for a fraction of a second, until the rider permits it. When he ultimately seeks to avoid discomfort by putting his head in the correct position, — *and then only,* — the hands must soften immediately and resume their light, normal feel. In the first instances, it is better to let the reins go slack when rewarding the horse's endeavor to carry his head correctly. This insures his associating the ideas of comfort and correct head carriage. Here again, the rider's degree of success will be determined by the speed and skill with which he detects the horse's efforts to shift his head to the proper place, and permits it by softening the hands.

Lowering a "Star-Gazer's" Head

To cite one example in applying the rule just given, relative to the action of the hands, take the case of a "star-gazer," (a horse which pokes his nose, head, and neck, high and stiffly in the air, the neck often being "upside down"). Most riders attempt to lower the head by carrying their hands low beside the horse's neck and futilely trying to pull the head down. Nothing could be more foolish. The horse, by tipping the head a little farther to the rear, or tossing it suddenly in any direction, can momentarily escape the tension of the reins, ("escape the bit"). Following the old rule of reward and punishment, he will, of course, continue throwing his head as long as he succeeds in escaping the annoyance of the bit, even though it be only for a moment. In other words, he is being taught by the momentary reward he receives, that his procedure is correct. (See Plate XL.)

The correct and logical way to lower the head of such a horse, is to hold the reins short enough, *(and no shorter)*, so that it is impossible for him, by any means, to escape the bit for a single moment. The hands, instead of being lowered in an attempt to pull the horse's head down, are raised, so that, as usual, the forearm and rein make a straight line. *The tension on the rein must become greater than in the normal feel. The hands are more or less fixed, and vibrations may be simultaneously employed, all of which increase the horse's discomfort.* The legs compel him to continue at the gait at which he is moving, while the hands steadily hold the head in its elevated position. Sooner or later, he becomes tired and uncomfortable in this strained position. Also, he soon discovers that the usual throwing about of the head permits no escape from the bit; and begins a search for a new way. Finally he will endeavor to lower it to a more comfortable and natural position. *Instantly the hand softens to permit the lowering.*

Plate XL *Horse "star-gazing." Reins too long; hands too low.*

The horse will doubtlessly make many efforts to raise his head again to its "star-gazing" attitude, but eventually will discover the futility of his efforts to escape the bit, which only acts more strongly when his head is elevated. Thereafter he will maintain the proper head carriage which gives comfort with a less disagreeable tension on the reins. With practice, a horseman can lower, by this means, any "star-gazer's" head in a few minutes. It will, however, often take a long time to redeem a bad case.

As usual, work first at the walk or slow trot, then at the faster gaits. Remember that the horse's impulsion and momentum are low at the walk; therefore a very slow trot, easy to sit, is often better, when trying to place the head or improve the mouth. The hands are more effectual when the rider sits quietly and firmly in place. Also, the horse's head remains still at the trot, which simplifies the work of the hands. Always have the hands so placed that they can pull the snaffle bit against the corners of the mouth. To do this, they should remain fairly high at all times when combatting a head carriage which is too high. They are instantly lowered to their normal position, of course, when the horse lowers his head.

With an inexperienced rider, the hands and arms may not be sufficiently quick and skillful to relax and follow the star-gazer's head downward when he first attempts to lower it. In this case, quickly opening the fingers and allowing the reins to slip through them, will insure the instantaneous reward, which is vital. The reins are promptly readjusted after the head goes down.

Violently Thrusting the Head Downward

A star-gazer will invariably go to a second type of defense, after once he has learned that he can escape heavy tension on the bit, by lowering his head. This usually consists in thrusting the head *violently* downward and out to the front. Do not correct this fault immediately, as success is surer and more rapid if the horse is taught one thing at a time. Moreover, the head should move down and out to the front, when the reins are loosened. It is only the *violent thrust* which must be stopped later. The solution is the same; make him uncomfortable as his head reaches the limit of its downward thrust. This is done by tightening the fingers of one or both hands, and fixing the hands, so that he receives a bump on the mouth from the bit, as a penalty for his violence. He soon comprehends that roughly thrusting his head downward is painful, and so tries extending it softly, and by degrees. To this desired movement, the hand gives.

All horses should be taught, at all gaits, as well as at the halt, to stretch out the neck and lower the head, when the rider's hands abandon the reins or lighten the normal feel. They should always do it gently; not brusquely. Also, whenever the horse is at rest, either halted or moving, a good horseman immediately relaxes his fingers and allows the extension and lowering of neck and head, which permits the horse to rest his neck, back, and loin. Patience and skill, and above all, thought, in following the principles of instantaneous reward and punishment, will succeed in making any horse with a faulty head carriage, take a normal feel on the bit, with head and neck correctly placed, — providing the horse is sound and has a fairly good disposition.

Regular Exercise

One point should never be forgotten in correcting vices, and during all training. Every horse of spirit must receive enough regular daily exercise to keep him calm, if training of any sort is to progress without battles, injuries, and loss of temper, — all of which, sooner or later, ruin a horse's mouth, legs, and manners. With difficult ones, give the first exercise on a longe,[23] or at liberty. With horses that have been poorly trained, or have bad mouths, a session will be required daily, just after mounting, for many weeks, before they will "accept the bit" properly. This is also true of horses with poor conformation.

---

[23] Longe. A long tape or rope attached to a halter-like head gear by which a horse can be exercised on a circle around the trainer. The head gear is called a "cavesson."

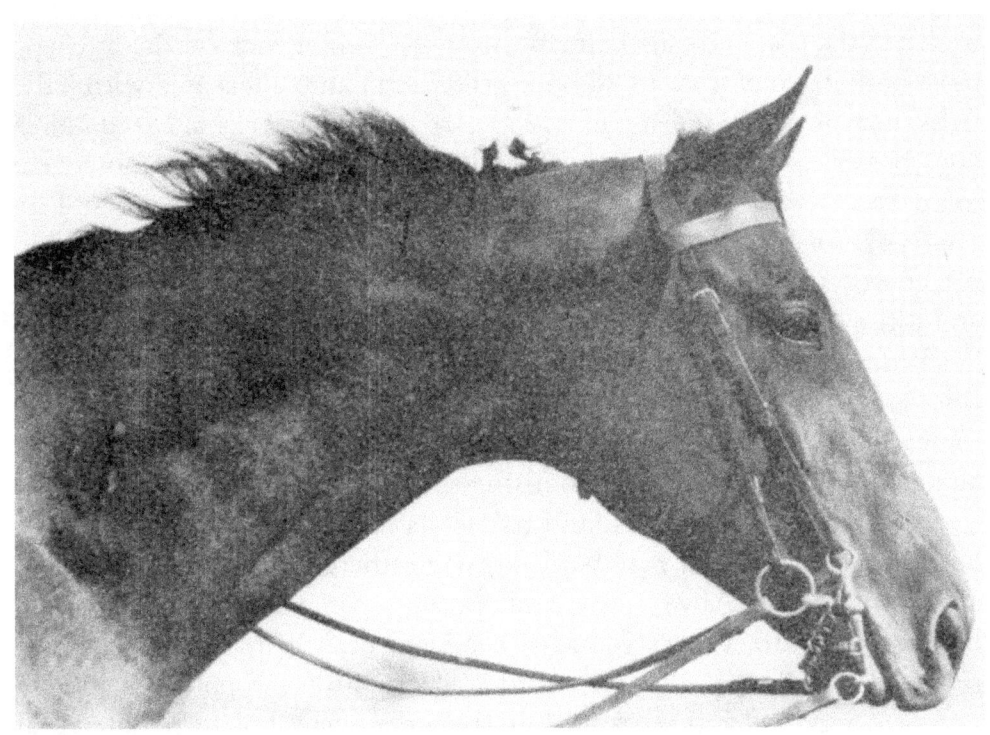

Plate XLI *Mild double bridle. Curb bit with short shanks and sliding mouthpiece.*

COMBINATIONS OF REIN ACTIONS

While vibrations, half-halts, and fixed hands were nominated as the normal means of defeating specific resistances, it must be realized that many horses combine two or more forms of resistance. For example, stiffening the jaw and throwing the weight on the rider's hands by lowering the head, are usually found together. Here, the combination of vibrations to soften the jaw, and half-halts to throw the weight back off the forelegs, must both be employed. In addition, the fixed hand, alternated with half-halts, may be used against a low head carriage in some cases. Fixed hands are a better cure than half-halts, for a low head. They will take more time to get results when first tried, however. Carry the hands forward and fix them in place, high and up toward the horse's ears, with a strong, unvarying resistance. An occasional half-halt will also help. This will become painful and ultimately make the horse seek escape for his mouth, by raising the head to a more nearly normal position. As has often been indicated, the rider's ingenuity and tact must come to his succor in analyzing and solving the various problems his horse introduces. Think over the enemy's tactics, and adopt the offensive plan promising success.

Vibrations, fixed hands, and half-halts may all be used with one or both hands. One hand may be fixed, while the other uses a half-halt or a vibrating effect. Always, the results sought for with any horse should be: first, the correct carriage of the head and neck, with the normal feel; second, relaxation of the jaw; third, relaxation of the poll. Adopt rein effects to accomplish those results, in the order given. It is to be noted that flexion, in a horse's neck, comes principally above the line where the reins pass the neck. As the flexion should be at the poll, never carry the hands low, on a horse which lowers his head and flexes the neck near the shoulders.

Oftentimes, in demanding flexion of the jaw, the amenable, well-made, young horse will flex his poll simultaneously, before the rider desires or seeks poll flexion. It results from what light fixing of the hands has been necessarily combined with vibrations, to accomplish the softening of the jaw. There is no disadvantage to this, so long as the jaw softens first; but flexion at the poll, before any softening of the jaw, occurs, should be avoided. If the horse does begin bending neck and poll before giving his jaw, lighten the hands, push him out on his bit at a freer gait. Then start trying again to flex the jaw, with very light "fingering" of the reins, after he has extended his neck.

Dismounted Flexions

Many great horsemen, particularly in the days when high-school riding was the principal form of equestrian sport, devoted much time to flexing the poll, jaw, and even the whole neck, while dismounted. Doubtlessly, these methods have some merit, *if properly executed by an expert,* but normally, it is believed that flexions can be secured just as well, mounted, and with a great saving of time. Once more, a caution is offered against over-doing flexions. In these days, speed and power, with all the liberty of head and neck possible, are necessary in the sports of hunting, polo, racing, and jumping. A horse cannot do his best work, or extend himself to his utmost, when flexed to an extreme, or deprived of the use of his head and neck, or "balancer." As a matter of fact, if a horse can be "rated" at all gaits, if he will turn and stop, and go quietly in company, what more is desired? Collection and flexion, when overdone or inexpertly used, militate against the above qualities.

The following method of defining, in a general way, the five effects of the reins, is that adopted by the United States Cavalry School, from the French Cavalry School at Saumur. These five effects are capable of an infinite number of variations, depending upon the exact amount and direction of the force applied, as well as upon the various combinations of effects employed. They are further modified by the actions of the rider's legs. Despite the numberless variations thus made possible, it is very useful to have a knowledge of how to produce these five effects, and of their results on the horse. With practice, their use, singly and in combination, ultimately becomes instinctive.

The effects of the right rein are used as examples throughout.

1. FIRST REIN EFFECT

"Opening" or "Leading Rein"

The opening rein is used to turn the horse to the right, from the halt or while moving at any gait. It is the rein effect with which a green colt can be most easily taught to change direction. As it acts in a natural, simple manner, it is one of the first employed. (See Sketch I).

The right hand is carried to the right and slightly to the front. There is no tension or pulling to the rear. It turns the horse's head and bends his neck to the right, throwing the bulk of their weight on the right foreleg. This tends to make him lose his balance to the right, and causes him to move in that direction to regain his equilibrium. If in motion, the horse turns to the right on a large curve, the body following naturally after the head and neck. When using this rein effect, the rider's two legs keep up the horse's movement, usually acting with equal force. However, if a rather sharp turn is desired, the right leg is used more vigorously against the horse's side, and a little farther to the rear. This pushes the hind quarters to the left more rapidly, and makes the curve over which he is moving, sharper. If the horse is at a halt, and the rider does not use his legs, this rein will simply turn the head to the right, and weight the right shoulder.

The left hand, normally passive, should be kept low. (Most riders pull on that rein or carry it across the horse's neck, which counteracts the effect sought with the right rein). If the horse bends his neck too far to the right, the left rein intervenes by being fixed at an appropriate length, low and close to the left shoulder, in order to limit the neck's bend to the right. This is often necessary with a green colt, and prevents his becoming "rubber-necked," (bending the neck too much at the shoulders, instead of uniformly throughout its length).

The effect of the opening rein is to lead the horse to the right front, not to pull him around. A common fault in riding is pulling when changing direction although no decrease in speed is desired.

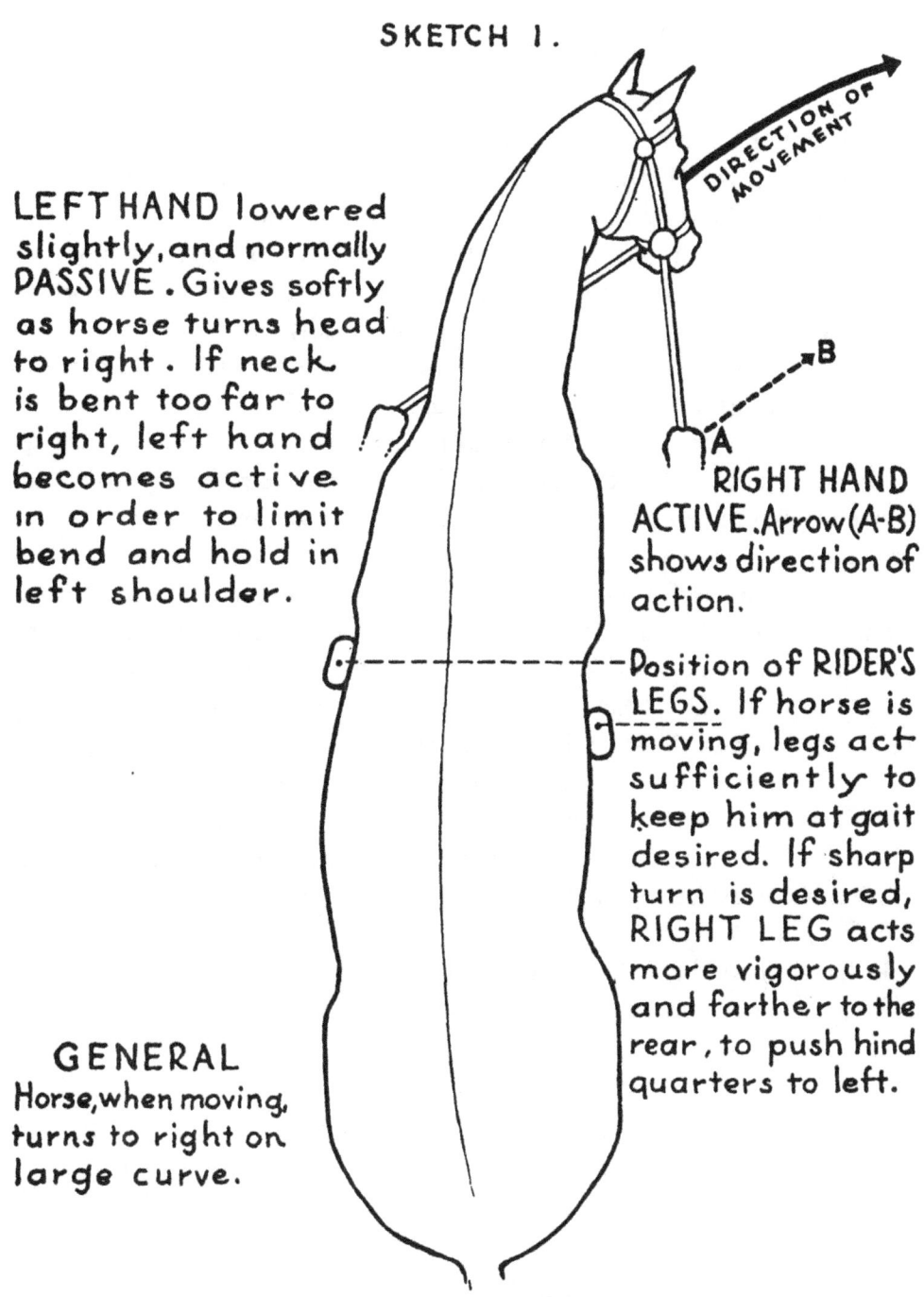

1st **REIN EFFECT**
Right Opening, or Leading Rein

2. SECOND REIN EFFECT

"Direct Rein of Opposition"

The right hand, held normally a few inches higher than the withers, is carried slightly to the right, and drawn to the rear, to a point where it becomes effective. The hand is then more or less fixed, thus bringing the horse's nose to the right and rear. The neck, perforce, bends to the right as a result, and the weight of the head and neck is thrown on the right shoulder. This weight impedes the action of the right shoulder and leg, and also breaks the horse's equilibrium to the right. Automatically his hind quarters are forced around to the left. If he is at a halt, the action will turn him about in place; — forelegs moving to the right, hind legs to the left.

If moving, the horse is forced to turn to the right. The sharpness of the curve is regulated by the amount of tension on the right rein. The hind quarters being forced out to the left, the turn is made, more or less, "on the forehand."

This is a powerful rein effect, and should be taught all horses, as it is irresistible when the right leg, or spur, if necessary, is used also to force the hind quarters to the left. The horse is compelled by these aids to turn very sharply to the right. When, through fear or obstinacy, he resists turning, this rein effect and the spur should be used.

The left hand, held above the left shoulder, gives passively to the front as the head turns to the right. It should not resist the action of the right rein, unless the horse bends his neck too far to the right, in which case the left rein becomes active, and limits, as necessary, the bend of the neck. (See Sketch 2). With a horse heavy on the forehand, and inclined to pull, the right hand should be well raised, in using this rein effect, to raise the head and decrease the load on the shoulders.

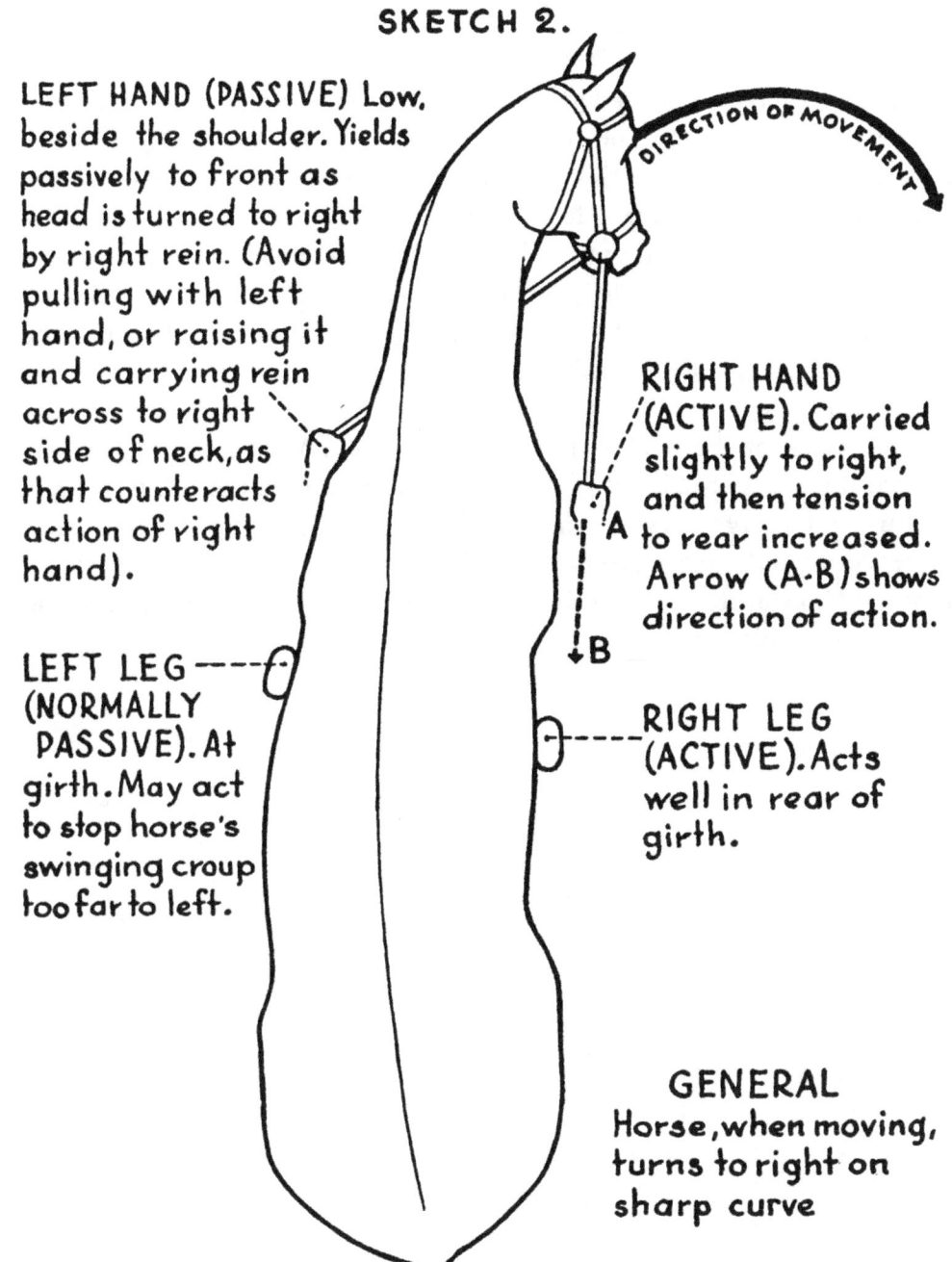

SKETCH 2.

LEFT HAND (PASSIVE) Low, beside the shoulder. Yields passively to front as head is turned to right by right rein. (Avoid pulling with left hand, or raising it and carrying rein across to right side of neck, as that counteracts action of right hand).

LEFT LEG (NORMALLY PASSIVE). At girth. May act to stop horse's swinging croup too far to left.

DIRECTION OF MOVEMENT

RIGHT HAND (ACTIVE). Carried slightly to right, and then tension to rear increased. Arrow (A-B) shows direction of action.

RIGHT LEG (ACTIVE). Acts well in rear of girth.

GENERAL Horse, when moving, turns to right on sharp curve

2nd REIN EFFECT
Rein of Direct Opposition

3. THIRD REIN EFFECT

"Bearing" or "Neck Rein"

The right hand is carried just over the crest of the neck, and acts toward the left front. The rein, to be effective, should bear against the right side of *the upper half of the neck,* as this part of the neck is more sensitive to the rein than that near the shoulders. It is an artificial effect, and not powerful, but is the one habitually used with trained horses, to change direction without changing speed, particularly in polo. By using the *left opening rein* in early training, and later combining the *right bearing rein* with it, obedience to the right bearing rein alone is easily taught.

It turns the horse's nose upward to the right, and forces the bulk of the weight of the neck onto the *left* shoulder. While its effect is not strong, if moving, the horse's balance is shifted toward the left front, and he turns on a large curve to the left. The rider's legs normally remain in place, acting only to sustain the gait. (See Sketch 3). The effect should be produced intermittently each time the left foreleg is moved, when working with a green colt.

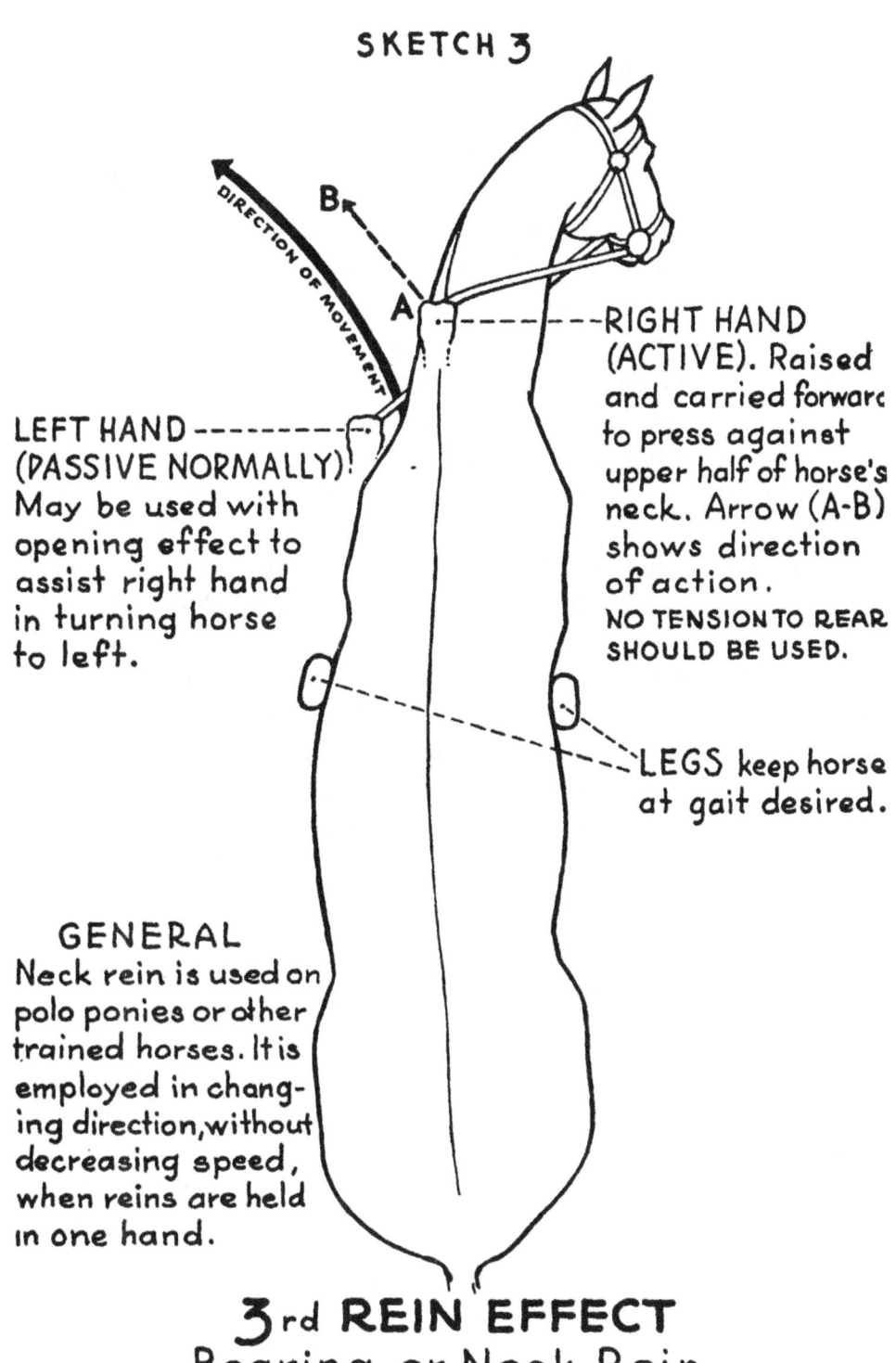

4. FOURTH REIN EFFECT

"Rein of Indirect Opposition, in Front of the Withers"

The right hand, slightly raised, is carried across the neck to the left, *in front of the withers,* and then tension is applied *to left rear.* (See arrow in Sketch 4).

The horse's nose is pulled to the *right and rear,* while the mass of head and neck are forced against the *left* shoulder, impeding its action and tending to break his equilibrium toward the left.

If the horse is standing still, *the rein of opposition in front of the withers* tends to push the shoulders around to the left rear, and the hind quarters, due to the movement of the shoulders, are automatically forced to the right front, the horse turning in place on his center.

If moving, the horse turns to the left, the sharpness of the turn being regulated by the amount of tension on the right rein. In turning sharply to the left, the left rein can also aid by acting to the left rear, and parallel to the right rein. As the horse becomes well trained, the left rein should become more and more passive.

The rider can force the horse to turn on his center by using his left leg to push the croup to the right. If, however, he is teaching a "turn on the haunches," the right leg acts well in rear of the girth to keep the haunches inside and prevent their swinging out on the turn. This rein effect is used to turn a trained horse when the reins are held in one hand, as in polo. (Sketch 4).

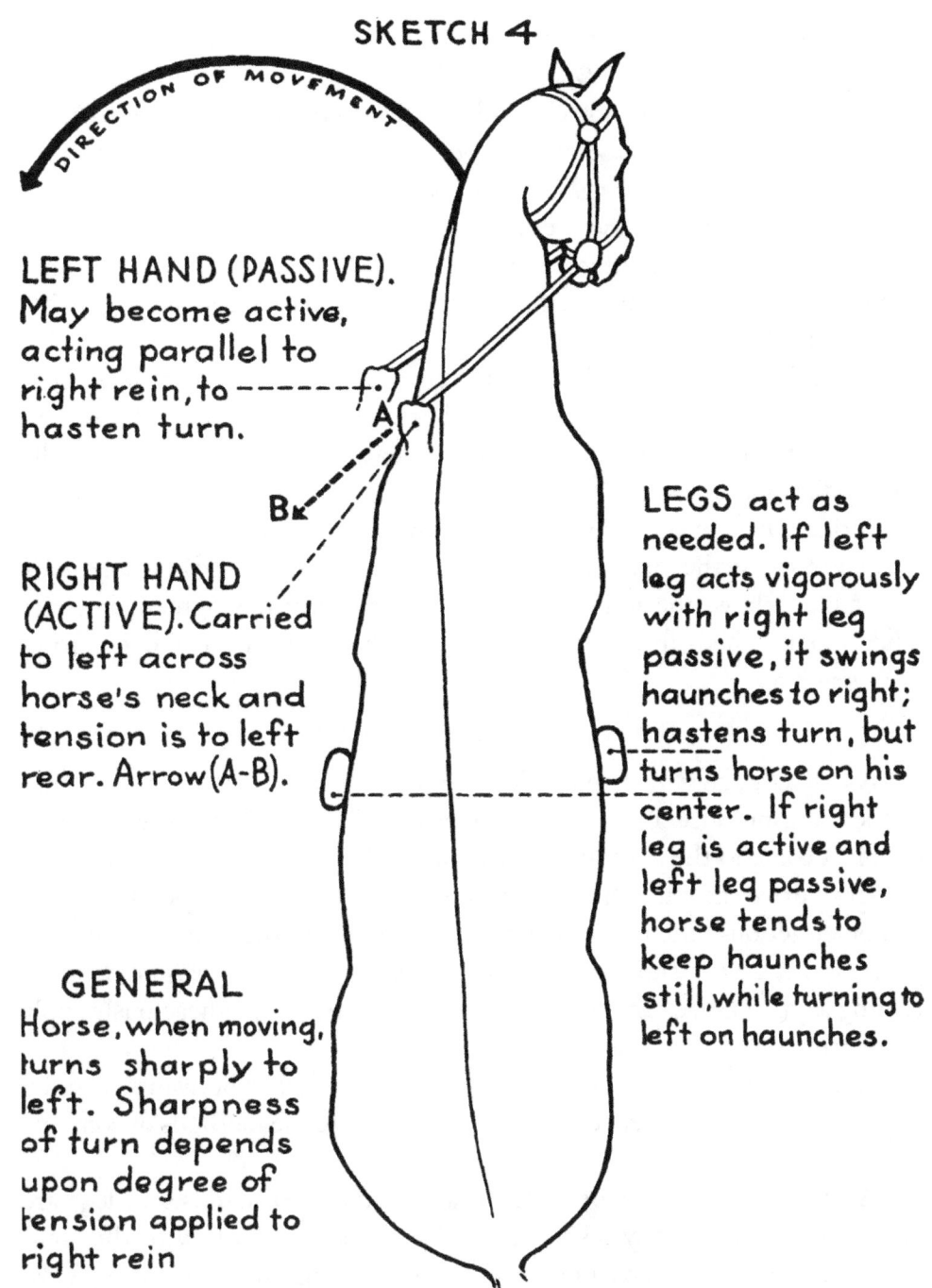

SKETCH 4

DIRECTION OF MOVEMENT

LEFT HAND (PASSIVE). May become active, acting parallel to right rein, to hasten turn.

RIGHT HAND (ACTIVE). Carried to left across horse's neck and tension is to left rear. Arrow (A-B).

GENERAL Horse, when moving, turns sharply to left. Sharpness of turn depends upon degree of tension applied to right rein

LEGS act as needed. If left leg acts vigorously with right leg passive, it swings haunches to right; hastens turn, but turns horse on his center. If right leg is active and left leg passive, horse tends to keep haunches still, while turning to left on haunches.

4th REIN EFFECT
Rein of indirect opposition (<u>in front</u> of the withers)

5. FIFTH REIN EFFECT

"Rein of Indirect Opposition, in Rear of the Withers"

The right hand is kept to the right of the withers, although the rein acts obliquely to the rear and left, toward the horse's left hip. The rider's right leg is active and helps drive the horse's hind quarters to the left. *His head is drawn to the right and rear; the neck and backbone are curved to the right, forcing the mass of the horse against his left hip and hind leg,* while increasing the weight borne by the left shoulder, as well.

The left rein is normally passive, but may act parallel to the right rein, or, more often, as a "leading rein, " (First Rein Effect), to assist in moving the horse to the left front.

The right leg, and right rein of indirect opposition, in rear of the withers, have a powerful, dominating effect. A moving horse, when "bent around the right leg" by their action, is overbalanced to the left, and must move diagonally to the left front crossing his front and hind legs respectively, to retain his equilibrium. It is impossible for a well-trained horse to resist their action, or to shy toward the right when these "aids" are applied. His whole body is bent like a bow, the rein and rider's arm forming the tightened string. When moving, he is forced to chase his own balance toward the left front. (See Sketch 5.)

Rein Effects; General Remarks

As stated, these five rein effects can gradually be merged, one into another, and produce an infinite number of different effects. The "passive" rein must come to the assistance of the "active" rein at times, and the rider's legs act to drive the haunches over to one side or the other, depending upon the horse's actions. The reins must be shortened or lengthened, as necessary. For example, a very short hold must be taken on the bearing rein, when training a green horse. The rein also must be shortened to efficaciously apply the "Fifth Effect."

Any horseman with theoretical knowledge of what he wants, can, by practice, master the rein effects, and soon appreciate the methods of combining them.

As a final item, let it be stated that all actions of hands and legs are intermittent, not a steady resistance with the rein, or push with the spur. Each time the horse yields a point, the rein or leg momentarily also yields. Then the action starts again, until the desired result is obtained, when legs and reins both immediately become passive.

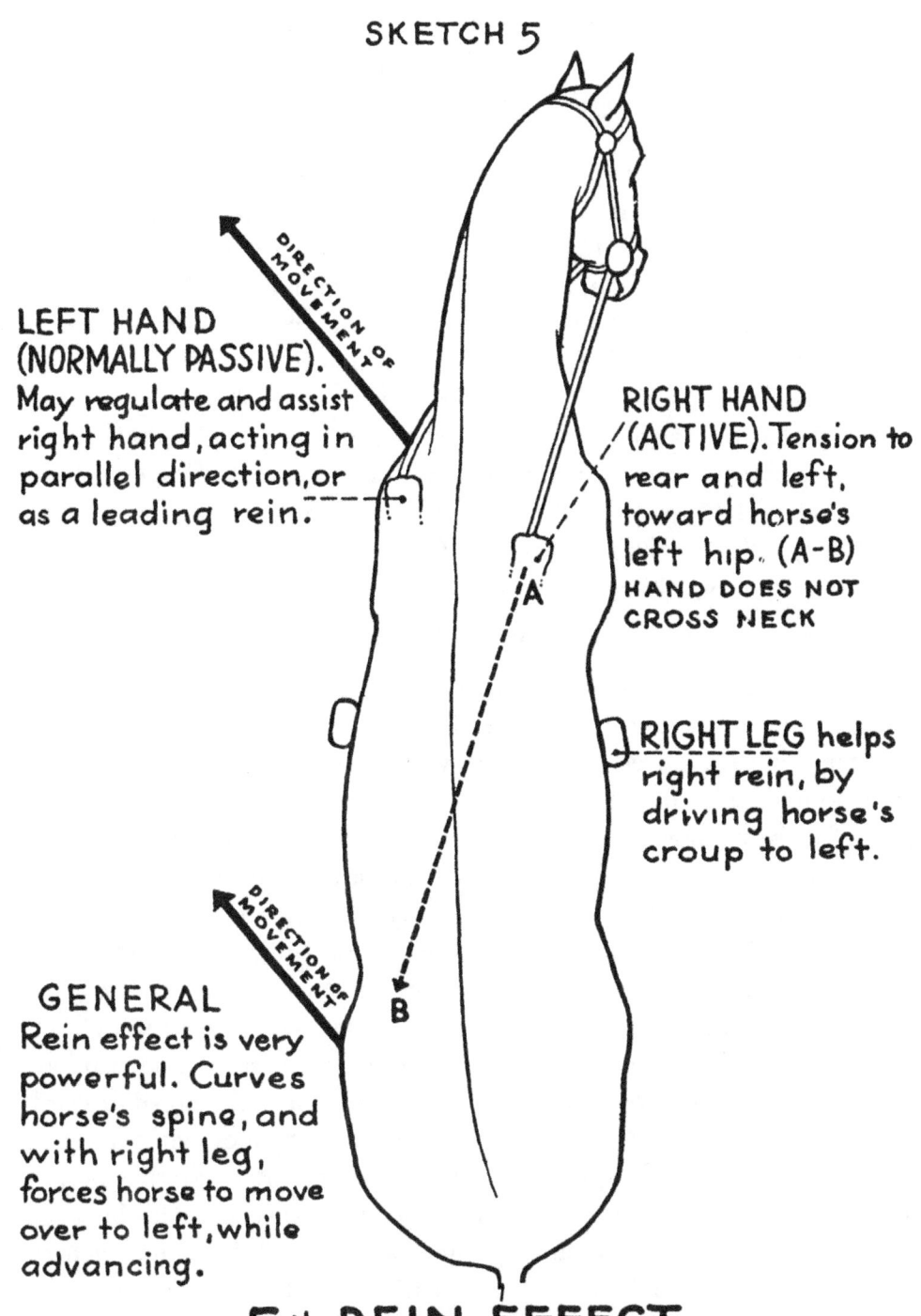

The Legs

The use of the legs as aids is not difficult to learn, yet the importance of their use cannot be overstressed. The expression "legs" is here used to indicate the leg from the knee down. Spurs are considered as part of "legs" in equestrian language.

Many riders make no progress as trainers, because they habitually carry their legs away from the horse's sides, or, in an equally useless manner, allow them to hang utterly inert. As was described under "The Seat," Chapter I, the calves normally should rest softly and continuously clinging against the horse's sides, with just sufficient steadying by the knee joints to prevent their swinging back and forth, or losing contact with the horse. (See Plate XXXII.) With the stirrup-straps perpendicular, and the heels well depressed, the rider's spurs are a few inches from the horse's sides, and *just in rear of the saddle girths*. During all work, every horse, by degrees, should be inspired with the greatest obedience to, and respect for, the legs. *The most important fundamental of training is to develop the habit of moving straight to the front in response to their combined action.*

Action of the Two Legs

When the two legs act together, the effect should be produced by squeezing the horse ahead with the calves. In case more force is needed, hard taps with the calves, or heels, (if without spurs), are employed. When these do not suffice to make him walk forward, if at a halt, or increase the gait or rate when moving, the spurs promptly come into action. The legs act against the horse directly from their usual position, without moving either to front or rear. The common error is to carry the legs too far rearward when using them. Their action back against the horse's flank, tickles and irritates him, often causing him to check his gait, switch his tail, or kick at the spur. Ordinarily, the spurs are brought into contact with the horse's sides by merely turning the toes farther outward. This gives the spurs a sideward and forward action, which the French refer to as "pinching the horse forward." The heels should remain depressed and lower than the toes, when using the spurs, which, as explained, keeps the calf muscles contracted, thus permitting the legs to squeeze powerfully. Occasionally, especially with long stirrup-straps used in breaking and training, it will be difficult to touch the horse's sides without raising the heels a trifle, but this should be avoided when possible, as it disturbs and deranges the seat. It is an easy and bad habit to acquire. Where a severe attack is called for, the legs are moved outward three or four inches, and the spurs brought energetically against the horse's sides one or more times, as necessary, just in rear of the girth. The force of the attack should be thoughtfully measured, as the amount of force necessary varies with the circumstances. The thighs and knees should remain fixed in place when using lower legs.

Spurs should have no rowels, except in those few cases where it is impossible to secure results without them. Such cases occasionally may be found when dealing with badly spoilt horses, which run backward, balk, or refuse to jump. A spur-shank with a blunt, ball-like end, which comes into contact with the horse's sides, is usually satisfactory. With sluggish individuals, it may be necessary to have a sharply squared end to the spur-shank. This will be severe enough to obtain results with almost any horse. The shanks should have sufficient length to permit the horse's being easily touched when occasion demands, without forcing the rider to raise his heels. This, of course, presumes that the rider is sufficiently experienced to avoid the grievous error often committed by beginners, of raising the heels and hooking the spurs into the sides of the horse, whenever he jumps an obstacle, takes a fairly rapid gait, or "plays up." Riders of this sort are not competent to wear spurs of any sort. A person with long legs needs a long-shanked spur, in order to use it without displacing the leg. The spur should be firmly strapped, so that it cannot slip on the boot, and so that its action will be always the same.

Thus, the action of the legs is always progressive in its intensity. It begins by squeezing gently with the calves, later reinforcing them by a touch of the spurs, or, in cases of flagrant disobedience, using them for a severe attack. The same principle, always applied in using the rein effects, is equally true in the use of the legs. The moment the horse responds, their action ceases. The moment he resists, their action is intensified. With a young horse in particular, the actions of the legs are intermittent. When he responds to their indications, even though the demands are not fully complied with, their actions diminish in force; or cease momentarily, being taken up again almost immediately, if need be, until their demands are fully met. This prompt reward for obedience quickly teaches deference to the legs, without which, no horse can be controlled, if, through a whim, he decides to assume command of the situation. The only serious defenses which a horse may possess, are those which result from not moving forward in response to the legs. Balking, rearing, and whirling for the stables, are examples. All are easily cured by teaching him to go forward when the spurs act.

Action of One Leg Alone

The effect of using one leg against the trained horse's side, is to push his hind quarters in the opposite direction. If not restrained by the reins, he will move forward while turning. If the action of the leg continues, and the reins do not intervene, his gait increases as he turns to the right, (assuming the right leg alone is used). When a single leg acts, for the purpose of pushing the croup in the opposite direction, it is moved slightly to the rear by increasing the flexion of the knee a trifle. This displacement of the leg should be very slight; not over an inch or two at the heel. In using one leg alone, the common fault is to slide it too far to the rear. It should act *toward the rear as well as sideways,* in "mobilizing" (pushing over) the croup in the opposite direction. This differentiates its action from that of the two legs acting together, which act *sideways and toward the front.* A green horse usually pushes against the spur when he first feels it, but will soon give way to its persistent action. In case a horse kicks at the leg's action, each kick should be instantly punished by a severe counter-attack with the spurs. Hold onto the pommel of the saddle, if necessary, to remain on his back, but riposte immediately to each kick made. This bad habit is soon stopped by this method.

General Remarks on te Action of the Legs

The legs normally act in a perfectly logical manner. If the horse, moving on a circle to the right, for example, tries to throw his hind quarters in toward the center of the circle, rather than carry himself true on the curve desired, the right leg acts immediately, with whatever force is necessary, to drive the croup and whole mass out to the left. This "sliding in, " or "falling over the shoulder" is a very common fault with poorly trained horses, and is often seen when they are rounding the corner of a show-ring. They effect this cutting-in on the circle, by throwing their weight on the inside shoulder and hip, turning the neck and head outward. The cure is found in using the Fifth Rein Effect, "Rein of Indirect Opposition, in Rear of the Withers," and the inside (right), leg, which bows the horse out to the left, and prevents his sliding in to the right.

It may be said that any horse ought to be trained before he enters the show-ring. Astounding as it may seem, there are, at our big horse shows, many Blue Ribbon winners in Hunter Classes, which no one could ride through a corner correctly, due to their low degree of training. They have never been taught to obey the legs, and know little about the rein effects.

It is always essential to bear in mind that the hind legs furnish all the motive power in the horse; that produced by the forelegs is negligible. Consequently, it is desirable that the hind legs move straight, and squarely in rear of the horse's mass, in order to most efficiently propel him along the line to be traversed. A horseman, therefore, should seek to keep his mount enclosed in the chute of the aids, formed by his two reins, hands, arms, and legs. When a horse, as a result either of not knowing how to accept the bit, or of a desire to escape its normal feel, tends to carry his croup to one side or the other, of the line on which he is moving, *he should be straightened by bringing his head, neck, and forelegs over in front of the hind legs*, rather than by pushing the hind legs sideways with one leg to a position in rear of his forehand. Pushing the croup sideways disrupts the gait and destroys part of the impulsion coming from the hind legs. Instead of being forced to accept his bit, he is slowed down, and assisted in avoiding it. If, for example, the horse persists in carrying his hind quarters to the right of his line of travel, the rider should squeeze with both legs, to maintain the impulsion, and use the left "Bearing Rein," or left "Rein of Indirect Opposition, in Front of the Withers," assisted, if need be, by the right "Opening Rein." These aids will tend to carry the forehand over in front of the croup, and at the same time, drive the horse forward into his bridle, without loss of impulsion or control. In other words, the hands and legs always should keep him moving straight ahead, in the frame formed by them, and maintain his free, bold movement in the direction desired. As has been mentioned, there should be much, work on a loose rein, but when the horse is "in hand," he should remain on the bit, and be constantly attentive. The better he is trained, the lighter his restriction in the frame of the aids becomes. He moves easily and contentedly, without attempting to escape.

The Weight

In many of the older books and manuals on equitation, the rider was instructed to lean backward, throwing his weight toward the rear, when decreasing the speed or halting. This was supposed to help the horse stop, by lightening the forehand and increasing the load on his hind legs. The supposition is erroneous. The rider should endeavor, at all times, to keep his seat fixed in balance, with his center of gravity approximately over that of his horse. As has been shown, the body must remain more or less inclined forward from the hips, under all circumstances, to accomplish these two things. Certainly, on a bucking horse, or during other violent behaviour, there will be times when the rider's entire effort will be required in staying on his mount. He must assume any position which will accomplish this. Aside from these occasions the body should never be allowed to fall out of balance, to the rear of the perpendicular. A trial will convince any open-minded horseman that his mount, either in polo or in hunting, will decrease his gait, check, stop, or turn more calmly, more easily, and more quickly if the forward seat is maintained. In performing most of these acts, the horse necessarily engages his hind legs well forward under his body, arching his back and loin a trifle in so doing, if he is handy, supple, and relaxed. The more forward the rider stays on the horse's shoulders which are his shock absorbers, thus freeing the back and loin, the more easily the work can be accomplished. The universal tendency is to fall to the rear, out of perfect balance. Very rarely is a rider seen leaning too far to the front.

THE VOICE AND WHIP

The horse quickly learns the significance of a few simple commands, such as "whoa," "trot," "gallop," and clucking. When calm, he will usually obey them. As a rule, outside of these commands, the voice conveys nothing, except by its tone and volume. Excited horses may often be calmed by low, soft words; while attentive ones may be stimulated to greater efforts by sharp, loud commands. When the horse is on the longe, or working at liberty in a pen or chute, the voice, and a whip with a long lash, are the principal aids.

A short riding whip is of great assistance in training a young colt, especially before he becomes familiarized with, and deferential to, the rider's legs. As a general proposition, however, to which there are few exceptions, the trained horse should be controlled and dominated by the hands and legs. When a whip is used, it involves partly abandoning, for the time being, the restraint of the reins, which, in turn, allows the horse to escape control.

A properly-schooled mount should be more afraid of energetic attacks by the rider's legs, than anything else in the world. He soon discovers that these attacks by the legs never are made, except when he is disobedient, and learns respect for, and prompt obedience to, their gentlest demands. This respect for the legs is built gradually, and as a matter of course, involves several unforgettable attacks with the spurs, at well-chosen, psychological moments during any horse's training.

JOINING THE BATTLE

When necessity demands, the rider should go to battle with spirit and determination, but always without loss of temper. The moment the horse gives in, admitting defeat, the tactful horseman is prodigal of his rewards.

Doubtlessly, some horses behave better when the rider carries a whip. If this is the case, one should be carried, but the legs and spurs should supplant it as rapidly as possible. In the horse's mind, the legs must represent supreme, indisputable authority.

Never urge the horse forward with the legs, and immediately, either by accident or intent, fall back on the reins, contradicting what the legs have asked. With a horse that balks, or is unresponsive to the legs, frequent frank and energetic attacks must be made with the spurs. During the attack, the saddle may be held with one hand, and the reins loosely held with the other. This precaution will prevent being unseated during the struggle, or jerking the mouth when the horse finally gives in to the spurs and moves forward. Once started forward, his pace should be accelerated by intermittently continuing the attacks, meanwhile patting him on the neck, and ceasing the leg action at each increase of speed. The intensity of the force used by the legs should be decreased as the horse learns to obey promptly. Above all, avoid jerking the mouth, or halting this type of horse, immediately after he has obeyed and moved to the front. If possible, battle should be joined where plenty of space is available.

Plate XLII *Well-trained horses, displaying calmness, boldness, suppleness, balance, and agility. Note forward seat and brace against stirrups, buttocks pushed well to rear.*

CHAPTER V

BITS

All breaking and early training should be done with a snaffle bit only. The reason is obvious; it is vitally important that the colt be taught to "accept his bit," and take a firm, steady "feel" on the rider's hands. Consequently, the mildest form of bit, the snaffle, should be put in his sensitive, unmade mouth. The feel will be nil to start with, but should become stronger as breaking and training progress. As previously emphasized, no effort should be made to make his mouth "soft" by causing him to relax the poll or lower jaw muscles, until he has been fully confirmed in extending his head and neck in a natural position, while supporting this frank feel on the snaffle. Normally, it takes about three months to confirm a totally green colt in accepting the bit, and "making his mouth" should only be commenced when he begins to actually "pull," or "go through his bridle."

Making a green colt eat his oats with a snaffle bit in his mouth for several days before he is ridden with a bridle, is a wise precaution. It tends to prevent his acquiring the almost incurable habit of putting his tongue over the bit, since it is impossible to eat unless he keeps it under the bit, in its proper place. Great care should be exercised in the adjustment of the snaffle. It should be sufficiently high in the mouth to bear firmly against the commissures, (corners formed by the upper and lower lips), pulling them up very slightly, due to its snug adjustment. It should not, on the other hand, be so snug as to cause an uncomfortable, heavy wrinkling of the flesh. If, through carelessness, the snaffle bit is allowed to hang too low in the mouth, a colt invariably, — and a trained horse very often, — will contract the deplorable habit of putting the tongue over the bit, sometimes allowing it to "loll" out of one side of the mouth. This destroys all chance of having a soft, pleasant mouth, unless corrected, and once contracted, correction is most difficult. When confirmed in the habit, the only resource is in tying the tongue in his mouth, which, at best, is unsightly and unsatisfactory. A good method of tying the tongue will be described at the end of the chapter. Putting the tongue over the bit is generally commenced in an attempt to escape the discomfort caused by hands that never relax, but pull continuously on the reins, keeping the tongue pinched without surcease.

The snaffle bit used in breaking a colt should be of the jointed, type. Another model has two or three little metal strips, an inch or so long, dangling from the joint of the mouthpiece. The colt is inclined to play with the "dangles" with his tongue, and, as a result, keep it in the proper place. The mouthpiece should be big in diameter near the ends, so as to present a large bearing surface against the colt's mouth. One type with the large mouthpiece is often referred to as "the German snaffle," having been employed at the German Cavalry School in Hanover. It usually has a hollow mouthpiece, making it light in weight. (See Plate XXVIII.) It is advantageous to have either rubber or leather guards at each end of the mouthpiece, which are circular in form. These prevent the bit's slipping through the horse's mouth when acting on one rein only, and also insure the lips against being pinched between the mouthpiece and the rein rings of the snaffle. There is no good reason for not using guards on all snaffles, since they keep horses amiable by softening the action of the bits.

After the colt has learned to carry his head well extended, and remain in contact with the rider's hand, the making of the mouth by flexing jaw and poll normally can be also accomplished by using only the snaffle bit. However, if he is too spirited and energetic, a snaffle with a smaller mouthpiece may be substituted, which acts more severely. In general, however, it is not the severity of bit, but rather, the tact and skill of the rider's hands, which, by their quick relaxation and yielding to all concessions of the colt, make and keep his mouth fresh and soft. Many sweet-dispositioned horses, particularly if they were destined to gallop in the company of others, will go best throughout their careers on nothing but the snaffle. And these same horses, (especially if they have light necks and fine throat lashes), will soon be over-flexed and ruined by the use of curb bits in unskilled hands. No apprehension need be felt about a colt's mouth because he pulls a little strongly on the snaffle when feeling gay, providing he keeps his neck firmly stretched out.

After the colt's poll and mouth have been softened, and he is confirmed in extending the neck and head at all gaits, while accepting a frank feel on the bit, the double bridle may be put on. This normally should be done at the end of four or five months. The double bridle should consist of a snaffle and a mild curb bit, the latter having a curb chain and lip strap. The snaffle must be of a smaller size than the "German snaffle" to make room for the curb, but by all means, a mouthpiece of small diameter, more closely resembling a wire than a bit, should be avoided. With the double bridle, the snaffle is adjusted exactly as has been described above. With a colt, it is well to begin with what is called the "half-moon curb," in which the mouthpiece is quite large in diameter and there is no port. The upward-curved mouthpiece gives the bit its name. The higher the port, in a curb bit, the more severe is its action on the horse's mouth. This is because the tongue normally rests beneath the bits, and serves as a cushion to lessen the pressure of the bit against the bars, which are part of the bones of the lower jaw. Through some freak of nature fortunate for horsemen, there exists a space of several inches on the horse's jaw-bones, between the incisor teeth and the molars. It is in this space that the curb bit acts against the bars. As these are covered by only a membranous skin, they are exceedingly sensitive. When a curb bit rotates in the horse's mouth, as a result of force applied by the reins to the ends of the bit's lower branches, the port turns up to a position more or less perpendicular to the bottom of the mouth. In this position, the tongue moves into the port, and its cushioning effect is greatly diminished, while the pressure on the sensitive bars in the interdental space is correspondingly increased. These facts account for the severity of a bit with a high port. (See Plate XLI).

The length of the lower branches of a curb bit also influences its severity, for, since the curb chain fixes the amount the upper branches can rotate to the front when tension on the reins pulls the lower branches to the rear, there is a powerful lever action which increases the force exerted against the jaw. The effect of the lever is, of course, increased by each fractional part of an inch added to the length of the lower branches. Horses that require long-branched bits with high ports almost invariably have had their mouths ruined by poor hands. However, if they will still go fairly well with such barbaric instruments of torture, it is safe to assume that they can soon be taught to go better on milder bits, if placed under the tutelage of some humane, tactful rider, with educated hands.

For breaking and training, it is usually much better to use a double bridle with the two mild bits, snaffle and curb, than to start out with some variety of Pelham bit. Later on, after having completed the making of the horse's mouth with a double bridle, it is generally wise to substitute some mild form of Pelham bit, such as a "half-moon," or one with a "Tom Thumb" mouthpiece. The latter allows the mouthpiece to slide up and down on the branches, over a distance of about half an inch. For polo or hunting, a Pelham usually works admirably. In both these sports, requiring sudden checking and turning, the snaffle is not sufficiently effective to stop a keen horse, or a very tired one. Almost without exception, horses will pull when greatly fatigued, and there are times when a bit of more severity than the snaffle will be necessary to stop quickly enough to avoid accidents. The type and severity of Pelhams vary greatly, and the sound rule is always to use the mildest bit with which the horse goes well, while keeping his neck and head stretched out. A more severe bit will flex him, and make control easier for a day or two, but grave difficulties usually will follow.

The rule for the adjustment of the curb is to have the branches stand at an angle of approximately forty-five degrees with the horse's jaw, when the reins are pulled taut. It is better to have this angle larger than smaller; in other words, have the chain as loose as possible. If the bit "falls through," so that there is no lever effect, due to a loose curb chain, no damage is done; but a chain too tight, causing the curb to "stand stiff," is so severe that the horse soon will become over-flexed and fretful, throwing his head, and seeking to escape in any way possible.

There are many oddly constructed, patented bits, and doubtlessly some are effective on some horses. In any event, if the riders *think* they are, it is a satisfying thought. Those ripe with experience usually conclude that there are no "get-rich-quick" methods of making a horse's mouth. Hackamores and other devices also may serve certain purposes, and perhaps aid in some phases of training, but when the pace and excitement run really high, *a well-bred horse must know how to accept pressure on the bit without fear, flex, and come back to the rider's hand.* To teach this, the only short cuts are found in the rider's skill and technique, which can speed training and the making of the mouth; or in those Heaven-sent qualities possessed by some horses, — good conformation and sweet disposition. *Spend the time necessary to train the colt and make his mouth correctly, and you will be repaid a thousandfold.*

When a horse has contracted the vice of putting the tongue over, or "balling it up" back of the bit, about the only solution is to tie the tongue in the mouth, making it impossible for him to pull it back from its proper position underneath the bit. A piece of cloth tape, about three-quarters of an inch wide, can be used for the purpose. Cut a transversal slit part way across the tape, and slip one end through the slit, forming a noose. The noose is put around the horse's tongue, and drawn as tightly as possible without cutting off blood circulation. The two ends are then run down and tied underneath the lower jaw, adjusting the tension so as to keep the tongue in its proper place.

Another method which is sometimes effective, and which does not involve the actual tying of the tongue, is as follows: tie a piece of tape to the snaffle bit at the joint of the mouthpiece, having the two loose ends of equal length, before putting the bridle on the horse. The two loose ends come out of the corners of the horse's mouth and are tied to the two cheek-pieces of the bridle, or to the noseband at the middle of the horse's face. The latter method is quite effective. It works most easily if a small hole is punched in the noseband, running one end of the tape through the hole, and tying it to the other.

CHAPTER VI

MARKS OF A TRAINED MOUNT

Briefly but comprehensively defined, a well-trained horse is one easy to control, alone or in company, through being readily responsive and obedient to the aids, under all probable circumstances. This implies that he also possesses the following characteristics: *calmness; long, low strides; boldness; relaxation and suppleness; balance and agility.* To a very great extent, all of these, if not naturally present, can be developed in any well-bred, well-made colt, by training.

Calmness

Calmness is the result of rational, systematic training, which, above all, permits the colt a correct, natural, and comfortable carriage of the head and neck. This carriage is produced by his successively passing through three phases of training, which, in turn, teach him: first, to accept his bit; second, to relax and flex his jaw and poll, as well as to bend his neck to the right or left in answer to the reins; third, to "place" his head, as a result of raising it and permanently flexing the neck at the poll very slightly. This placing of the head improves his balance and appearance, and facilitates control by the hands.

During the first, or breaking, phase, the colt is taught by degrees to take a frank feel on the bit at all gaits, while carrying his head and neck well extended, and in a fairly low position. Carrying his head low allows his back and loin comfort and freedom, as they gradually become hardened, and accustomed to the rider's weight. In this phase, he is not taught to flex jaw or poll, but rather, is encouraged to stretch the reins fearlessly by extending his neck and head far out at all gaits, and taking a "good feel" on the bit. The hands remain passive to the greatest possible extent consistent with control. Some colts with well-put-on necks and nicely attached heads, relax and flex poll and jaw, without any preparatory exercises on the rider's part, as soon as additional tension is put on the reins to slow the gait, turn, or halt. However, the longer and finer the neck is, the more care must be exercised to avoid over-flexing or making a "rubberneck," (one too flexible and limp just in front of the shoulders). During the first phase, the colt is taught to walk, trot, or gallop, with long, free strides, to turn on wide curves, and to halt. Calmness, free strides, and strength are the principal objectives. He is allowed to carry himself as he pleases, providing he does not raise his head to an unnatural position. To correct this fault, see "Lowering a 'Star-Gazer's Head," see Chapter IV.

In the second phase, beginning usually after about three months' work in the first, the jaw is relaxed by vibrations, moving on circles, frequent changes of gait, "shoulder-in," and other similar exercises, which call for "fingering" the reins, and fixing the hands very mildly, and for short periods. After a few weeks' work of this sort has succeeded in softening the jaw, the poll is next relaxed by direct flexion, and by much practice in slowing and increasing gaits, changing gaits, and halting. While poll and jaw are being softened, infinite care should be exercised not to develop a permanently over-flexed neck. On the contrary, the desire and habit of fully extending neck and head with calmness, the moment the hands become passive, and of willingly taking the normal support on the bit, should be thoroughly instilled in the colt during this phase.

During the third phase, after having developed a fairly good mouth in the first two, the type of work just described in the second phase is continued, and in addition, much riding over varied ground should be done. Through all this, the young horse adjusts his equilibrium to the rider's weight, and raises the neck and head of his own desire, as he finds his balance, and his strength increases. He also acquires a very slight, permanent bend at the poll, when the reins are stretched, as his nose comes in a trifle from its earlier "poked out" position, characteristic of the green colt. At the end of this phase, he has a good mouth, is balanced, and his head is "placed." None of this work should be rushed. After it is thoroughly done, if the colt has nothing fundamentally wrong with his conformation which makes his work painful, and if his inherited disposition is good, he will have cultivated calmness. If well-ridden thereafter, and if allowed to carry his head and neck comfortably extended, he will usually remain calm. Almost without exception, it is the horses which have over-flexed, "upside-down," or otherwise distorted necks, that are fretful, unmanageable, and "runaways."

Plate XLIII *Teaching young horse to extend trot with neck and head stretched out while taking frank support on bit; reins a trifle too long.*

Long, Low Gaits

In hunters, polo ponies, chargers, and other riding horses used for practical work or sport, the desirable characteristics of efficiency and speed, necessary for supremacy, come from long strides, moving parallel to the direction of movement, and close to the ground. Such strides eliminate the unnecessary, ruinous pounding of feet, and the wasted energy inherent in high, short strides. The higher the horse's head is raised, the higher the feet are automatically raised, and the more all joints of the legs are flexed. So, here again are found cogent reasons for training with methods that will inculcate and encourage the horse to go at all gaits with head and neck naturally extended; since that attitude permits long, free, effortless strides. An additional reason for allowing great liberty of head and neck is manifest, when it is realized that the horse employs the gestures made by them to assist in all his movements, precisely as a man uses his arms in running, dodging, jumping, (see Chapter VII,) and recovering his equilibrium. Those gestures also help greatly in absorbing the heavy shocks and strains thrown on the tendons and joints of the forelegs, when jumping, or moving at fast gaits. The more difficult the country traversed, and the higher the jumps encountered, the more essential it is to give this liberty, in order that your mount may take care of you and himself. Your judgment should regulate his speed prior to reaching either bad ground or an obstacle, but once there, as well as for several moments during the immediate approach, you should give him his head, maintaining, with elastic arms and hands, only the lightest feel on his mouth, thus allowing his ability and judgment to govern while crossing. This oftentimes tests the rider's nerves and coordination, for every instinct urges him to grip the reins and tighten the arms, the exact opposite of what should be done in such circumstances. In bad places, the rule to follow is: *tighten the legs and soften the hands*. The ridiculous idea that a horse can be "picked up" when he stumbles, or assisted over the jump by the reins, merits no discussion. "Rated" and collected by the hands if and when necessary, before reaching any difficult obstacle or ground, — yes; but while actually passing over or across, or when regaining his partly lost balance, — no; *give him his head*. The fact that his gaits are free and his strides long, will not increase his liability to fall, after he has been balanced by work and training, regardless of certain misconceived ideas on the subject. Practice, and the instinct of self-preservation will insure his taking care of himself, if not annoyed and interfered with by nervous, apprehensive hands.

Efficient strides are cultivated in always pushing a horse tactfully ahead, particularly at the walk, by use of the legs, or, if need be, the spurs. Never let a colt loaf; make him move ahead energetically.

The extended trot and gallop are very beneficial exercises in developing long strides. Increasing the speed should be gradually and calmly executed, and the hands must permit the head and neck to stretch to the front by keeping shoulders, elbows, and hands elastic and passive. The well-trained horse takes a firmer support on the bit as his speed becomes greater, and yet his head and neck must be allowed to extend farther to the front. Thoughtful tact and skill with the hands are necessary to accomplish this, and to teach it to the horse. It is most easily accomplished by lightening the feel on the mouth *before* the speed is increased. *After* the horse extends the neck to the correct position, the speed is increased, and a stronger feel, required by the faster gait, is then taken on the mouth.

Many trainers spend hours working on circles, serpentines, and figures-of-eight, in order to develop "handiness." Some of this work is highly essential, but it tends to shorten the strides. Much more time than is usually devoted to it, should be spent in work on straight lines, changing gaits, and increasing and decreasing speed, with frequent halts interspersed. This cultivates longitudinal flexibility, obedience, and balance. Most difficulties in control arise from impetuosity, and the desire to keep going; so a colt must be given much practice in slowing down and halting.

When working at the slower gaits, the rider's legs, (or spurs, if need be,) should be constantly in use, urging the horse to lengthen his strides. The legs of the rider, if efficient, do much toward making the legs of his mount efficient. Many riders fall back, pulling on the reins for support, the moment their horses increase the gait unexpectedly. Others urge them forward with voice and legs, and when they move out, as asked, fall back on their mouths, putting them "between the devil and the deep blue sea." Both types bump the mouths, and make their mounts afraid of their bits, and, as a consequence, they soon lose boldness and length of stride. *By contrast, a good rider, when his mount unexpectedly increases the gait slightly, instantly relaxes his arms and fingers for a moment.* He then adjusts his seat and balance, after which he very softly collects the reins and regulates the gait. His horse is never afraid to accept the bit or lengthen his strides in response to the call of the legs or spurs.

Often, if the rider will lean farther to the front when he thinks his horse is pulling, he will discover that he, himself, and not the horse, is at fault. The horse is simply trying to extend his head, and seems to be "pulling," to the rider, who is partly supporting himself by the reins, as a result of being out of balance and behind the horse. Thus it is evident that accidentally or unknowingly falling against the bit, and riding out of balance by leaning too far to the rear, inevitably make a horse shorten his strides, and ruin his mouth.

Boldness

Courage is largely an innate quality. Yet a colt, not instinctively bold, may have this virtue greatly developed through proper training. Again, as in teaching long strides, *the rider's legs are the principal means of inspiring boldness.* Through being driven ahead tactfully and continually by the legs, during all his training, a horse finally arrives at the state where he moves to the front as a reflex, when the legs or spurs are used, regardless of what faces him. A timid horse, if not trained to respond to the legs, is forever worthless. A well-disciplined horse although by nature timid, is so inescapably framed in the reins and legs, that he ultimately accepts that fact without serious resistance, and habitually obeys the rider's aids. Since no horse ever becomes a machine, there will be occasional struggles, but they will grow less and less intense, if the horse is ridden well. Always, throughout a horse's career, the trainer's legs must attack with great vigor, if need be, to drive him straight forward into the narrow path laid out by the reins.

In developing boldness, tact and common sense play their part, as in all else. As the days go by, the youngster must be ridden across increasingly difficult terrain, but only as he becomes easily manageable, and after he has been prepared, mentally and physically, by previous lessons. Never ask anything new or difficult from a horse, for which he has not been prepared. Demand only that which it is reasonably certain he can be compelled to do, without injury to his morale or legs. Having initiated something new, the rider should carry it through, unless he realizes, after having undertaken the job, that his judgment has been poor, and that the task is beyond the colt's ability. In that case, it is better to frankly admit the blunder, and wait until the horse is better prepared. It is, of course, bad for discipline to give up after demanding something unusual, but caution may be the better part of valor, in some cases. Often, a stubborn person persists in forcing a horse to try a feat beyond his powers. The consequences are always harmful to the horse, whose common sense in the matter has exceeded that of his rider. There are always times when any horse of spirit rises in defiance of authority. If what is demanded is within his ability, he should be forced, at all costs, to obey. If each progressive step in training has followed a more simple one, the foundation will be sound, and the rider, as a rule, can easily enforce his will when rebellion occurs. *Boldness will be born of obedience to the master's hands and legs; particularly the legs.*

GENERAL RELAXATION AND SUPPLENESS

General relaxation is simply a by-product of correct training. It should be cultivated for the first few minutes after mounting, each time the colt is ridden. Always start the day's work slowly, relaxing the jaw as a first step. Simultaneously, endeavor to take the "kinks" out of his back, while walking or slow-trotting on circles. This is done by bending his neck and entire spine uniformly, throughout their length, so that they coincide with the curve of the circle on which he is moving. The inside rein, using the Fifth Rein Effect, and the inside leg, accomplish this work of suppling the back and neck laterally. The horse is "bent around the rider's inside leg." Work off a horse's first ebullition of spirits on circles, serpentines, figures-of-eight, and curves, every day, if he is of an impetuous, high-spirited nature. As soon as the jaw, poll, and spine are relaxed and supple, proceed to training involving work at higher speed.

The longe and cavesson are most valuable in calming and suppling a high-spirited colt or horse. Work him for an hour, if necessary, on the longe; if after that, only fifteen minutes are spent in riding him, more will be accomplished than if the entire hour and fifteen minutes are spent on his back, without previous work on the longe. Many fights will be avoided through calming the horse in this manner, before mounting.

After decontracting jaw, poll, and back, start the schooling on straight lines and large curves, increasing and decreasing the speed, changing gaits, halting, and backing. Whenever feasible, an old horse should receive a little of this same sort of work each time he is ridden. Some horses, even after being trained, will always require many of these relaxing exercises, while others will need few. It is a matter of disposition and temperament, but in any case, an effort to "soften" and supple a horse always should be made immediately after mounting.

Never back a colt until he "takes his bit" frankly, and flexes perfectly. Backing should be done with slow, cadenced steps; no "running back" to avoid the bit should be tolerated. Keep his head low, and your weight well forward. Reward each step by softening the hands momentarily. Keep the legs against the horse's sides to check any hurrying, or deviation of the croup. The hind quarters are lightened by lowering the head, which makes backing easy for the horse. Raising the head cramps his loin, weights the hind quarters and renders backing painful, especially for a colt, with undeveloped back and loin muscles.

The sort of work just mentioned brings about the suppleness and relaxation which make control easy, and teaches the pupil to perform his tasks good-naturedly, *and with a minimum of effort.* Many special exercises, such as work on "two-tracks," "shoulder-in," "changing leads," "mobilizing the haunches," "turns on the forehand and hind quarters," and "galloping false," which are used in training, but which space does not permit describing, are of inestimable value in producing relaxation and suppleness. Certain exercises are valuable in correcting faulty habits of carriage or movement, and in breaking up certain vices. Unfortunately, many people think these exercises are an end for which to work. They are merely a means for developing, in the end, a pleasant, obedient, and supple horse.

Balance and Agility

All the schooling just described, also improves balance and agility. Nothing, however, can compare with systematic work across all types of country, for giving a horse the ability to shift his balance back and forth between his fore and hind legs, as occasion demands, and to use his feet with that cleverness which makes him safe to ride across any terrain.

Jumping little streams and fences, climbing and descending hills, and moving fast over difficult country, are most beneficial exercises. Allow the young horse to do this work half the time on a loose rein, picking his own way, and the other half on a stretched rein, under close guidance. Following an older, well-trained horse across country, immeasurably speeds and facilitates a colt's training. Since horses are inveterate mimics, the older one's dignified demeanor always will be imitated, to a great extent, by the youngster following. Going quietly in the company of other horses, without trying to forge to the front, is a matter of training and habit, which should be carefully taught the colt as soon as he is well broken.

This outline of characteristics desirable in a well-trained mount, and the general indications of how to secure them, are necessarily brief, as a detailed treatise on training would mean a book in itself.

Plate XLIV   *"Tanbark." A superb jumper, working on longe*

CHAPTER VII

Jumping the Horse at Liberty

Any horseman who has had the aesthetic thrill of watching an experienced horse soar over obstacles, when at liberty, has been furnished with a clue as to how a jumper should be ridden. The ease and grace with which he clears formidable fences, when unhampered by a rider, convincingly demonstrates that he requires the greatest amount of freedom the man on his back can possibly give him.

The Forward Seat described in Chapter I is perfectly adapted to use in jumping. With it, the rider's weight is distributed so that it interferes to the minimum extent with the horse's movements. Also, when riding over obstacles, it is easy to maintain a mechanically correct position which will keep the rider's weight so placed as to cause the least possible amount of inconvenience to the horse.

Effect of Shortening the Stirrups

When jumping obstacles higher than three and a half feet, the stirrups should be shortened from one to four inches; the higher the jumps are, the shorter the stirrups should be. It will be remembered that this involves the following modifications in the Seat:

The knees are raised and moved the least bit farther forward on the saddle-skirts.

The thighs are raised and consequently form a smaller angle with the horizontal.

The buttocks and trunk are pushed farther to the rear.

The trunk is inclined farther forward from the hips, in order that its center of gravity, which has been moved backward, will remain, as usual, over a point in advance of the center of its base of support. (Since the seat is out of the saddle much of the time when jumping, it will be recalled that the horizontal measurement of the base of support extends from where the inside of the knee is in contact with the saddle, to the heel of the boot.)

Roughly speaking, the body's center of gravity should be approximately in a vertical plane passing just in rear of the knee joints. (See Plate XXIV.)

The most common faults found in beginners, when the stirrups are shortened, are the following:

The knees are too high and pushed too far to the front. As a result the buttocks slide too far forward. In some very bad cases, the knees rest at the front ends of the saddle-skirts, or beyond them.

The heels are high: resulting from the faulty positions of the buttocks and knees.

The stirrup straps are not perpendicular.

The loin and back are humped.

All these faults make the seat weak and insecure. They result from failure to keep: the heels driven far down; the calves closed against the horse; the knees held in against the saddle-skirts; the back and loin muscles contracted sufficiently to keep the back straight and the loin concave. Any one of the above faults entails the others. (See Plate XLV.)

How the Horse Jumps

Before describing how the seat functions, and the manner of conducting the horse to, over, and beyond the jump, a brief discussion, from a mechanical viewpoint, of the horse's normal actions when jumping will be given. An animal with a short neck, such as a deer or dog, when jumping a high fence, pops almost straight up into the air, and lands on all fours simultaneously. A horse, on the contrary, by using his head and neck as a balancer, describes a graceful parabola, with his fore feet coming to ground well in advance of the hind. *It is an interesting fact that the fore feet strike the ground and leave it again before the hind feet touch.* Inasmuch as this see-saw, or bascule, movement is accomplished as a result of the employment of the head and neck, the necessity for the rider's not interfering with their movements during a jump, is evident. All have seen a poor rider hanging onto the reins and pulling the horse's head high in the air, over the top of a jump. With his neck thus immobilized, the poor horse also lands on all fours simultaneously, and is said to "jump like a deer."

Head and Neck, During Approach

In approaching an obstacle, a horse that jumps in good form, lowers and extends his neck in an easy, graceful position, in order to estimate the character and height of the obstacle, as well as his point of take off. Very often he may be seen extending his neck and head far to the front with a very swift gesture, just before his front feet leave the ground. This gesture apparently is made for the purpose of producing a counteracting force to the rear, permitting him to check and shorten his last strides in placing himself for his take-off. Also, with an extended neck, he can exert its greatest force in its next and important gesture. *Thus, during the approach, the rider's hands should be passive and exceedingly elastic, softly following all the forward and backward movements of the horse's head.*

Head and Neck, During Take-off

Just before raising his forehand, the horse throws his head and neck upward, placing their mass more or less directly over the shoulders. This is an advantageous position, since it is the powerful opening of the previously closed shoulder joints, that furnishes the principal muscular force in lifting his forehand. In addition, the momentum given the head and neck by the upward gesture tends to pull the forehand up in the first stage of its ascent. In this phase, the head and neck are used just as a man uses his arms in making a standing high jump. Here again, the reins in no way should impede the action of the head and neck. Often they will go slack, due to this rearward gesture, and since the jump has begun, it is well if they do. Poor riders bring the hands in to the body at this phase, pulling the mouth and greatly hindering the horse's efforts. They explain it as "lifting the horse;" by intelligent horsemen, it is more accurately termed "strangling."

Head and Neck, During Period of Suspension

Let the neck be considered as a lever between the shoulders and head. As soon as the forelegs are raised and start passing over the obstacle, the neck and head, (already across), are extended and thrust forcefully downward by a muscular effort of the neck. This exerts a counter force upward at the other end of the lever, which helps lift the shoulders and forelegs over the obstacle. The inertia of the head gives the muscles of the neck a point of support in exerting their force. This, perhaps, accounts for the fact that many excellent jumpers have rather large heads. Obviously, it is very important that the head and neck, in making the downward gesture to help the forelegs over, be hindered in no way by the reins.

Meanwhile, the hind legs having been engaged well forward under the belly, the hocks and other joints extend and propel the horse's entire mass upward and forward. As the hind feet leave the ground, the period of suspension begins. Immediately after the forelegs have cleared the obstacle, the head and neck are abruptly raised from their lowered position. A similar phenomenon to that produced by the downward gesture occurs; the muscles of the neck act against the inertia of the head as they swing it upward, and the counteracting force at the other end of the neck drives the shoulders downward. It is also this force that gives the horse a see-saw motion about his center of gravity, sending his fore feet to the ground well ahead of his hind ones.

Since the horse is entirely in the air at the time the head is thrown upward, the same interior muscular forces which drive the shoulders down, react again through a second lever, the body, and lift the hind quarters up. This second reaction greatly assists his clearing the obstacle with the hind legs, which are also being flexed and tucked up at the same time. *It is most essential that the rider stay out of the saddle at this phase of the jump.* Settling into it as the hind legs are clearing, inevitably destroys the effect toward raising the hind quarters, produced by the neck's gestures, and often knocks the hind legs down into the obstacle.

HEAD AND NECK, DURING LANDING

When landing, several other gestures are made by head and neck to soften the shock to the forelegs, as well as to raise them in their quick hop made to clear the way for the hind feet, which come to earth a fraction of a second later. For a detailed study of the horse's gaits and the effects produced by the head and neck, "Les Allures, le Cavalier" by L. de Sévy, is highly recommended.[24] M. de Sévy made several other profound studies of the movements and reactions of the horse and rider.

With this mental picture of the horse's movements during a jump, and with a knowledge of the importance of the gestures of head and neck, certain conclusions will be drawn regarding the corresponding actions desirable on the part of the rider.

PREMATURE JUMPING

No attempt should be made to ride a horse over obstacles until he understands and readily obeys the Aids. First and foremost, he should accept the bit, or in other words, "go nicely on the hand." Secondly, he should be easily controllable at any speed. Many trainers, unfortunately, start jumping their horses, and even entering them in horse shows, before they can be ridden at a gallop around a definitely prescribed circle. Potentially marvelous jumpers soon become unmanageable and are ruined for the hunting field or the show ring, by this illogical procedure.

---

[24] Librarie Legoupy, 5 Boulevard de la Madeleine, and Librarie Chapelt, 136 Boulevard Saint-Germain, Paris, France.

Horse "on the Hand"

When the horse is "on the hand," he necessarily must be "in front of the rider's legs," otherwise he can-not be kept "on the hand." This signifies that he is instantly responsive to the legs, increasing the gait smoothly and gradually at their demand. He carries his head fairly low and the neck well extended, accepting the frank feel of the bit calmly and without pulling. To his rider, he feels thoroughly committed to the forward movement at all times. If the rider increases tension on the reins, and squeezes with the legs at the same time, the horse remains calm while thus more tightly enclosed by the hands and legs. He cannot stop as long as the legs or spurs urge him ahead. The rider has the sensation that the horse's center of gravity is near his shoulders and always in front of the rider's legs. There is a slight preponderance of weight on the forelegs, which causes him to seek support on the bit.[25] At the free gallop, if the horse is a good jumper, the normal feel is a fairly strong one. Remember that the feel increases in intensity as the speed increases.

On the other hand, a horse "back of the bit" and legs gives his rider exactly the opposite impressions. He seeks to avoid a frank feel on the bit. The rider senses that the horse can stop or slow the gait with ease, and that the Aids are almost powerless to prevent it. His center of gravity seems to be back of the rider's legs, and his head raises or is tucked in at any increased tension on the reins, in an effort to avoid the bit. At any time, this horse can refuse a jump, or "fade back of the legs and bridle," out of control. It is impossible to ride such an untrained mount over difficult jumps, or any place else, unless through his own good will he chooses to go.

The Four Phases of Jumping

Riding over obstacles may be divided, for the purpose of discussion, into four stages: the approach; the take-off; the period of suspension; the landing.

Riding, During Approach

The approach may be considered as extending approximately over the last twenty yards prior to the jump. It is in this space that the rider has most opportunity to exercise his equestrian skill. He must have determined

---

[25] Horses, at speed, namely when racing, hunting, or jumping, carry a preponderance of their weight on the forehand, and should take a frank support on the bit. Well-trained horses at slower gaits keep their weight more equally distributed between the for and hind legs; consequently, they take much less feel from the hand than when going at speed. Highly collected horses carry a preponderance of weight on the hindquarters by engaging the hind legs well under the mass. They therefore take an exceedingly light feel on the bit. However, an exceedingly light mouth is greatly different from that of a horse "behind the bit." The former is "in front of the legs"; the latter "behind the legs."

the proper speed, and rated his horse accordingly. The proper speed will be governed by the size of the obstacle, the nature of the ground in front of it, other obstacles or hazards beyond it, and the speed with which the particular horse jumps best. In addition, certain horses jump much better when galloping with a particular leg leading. In approaching a formidable obstacle, if the time permits, the horse should be put on the lead with which he jumps best. Of these problems, the most important is rating the horse at the proper speed without annoying or exciting him. This takes delicacy and skill with the hands. Briefly, a combination of vibrations and momentary fixings of the hands are generally most successful. Above all, avoid leaning backward out of balance and pulling. About fifteen yards from the obstacle, rating a horse or bothering his mouth in any way should entirely cease. If, up to this point, increased tension and work with the hands has been required to slow the speed, it should from now on be stopped, and the normal feel smoothly and progressively established.

During the last few yards of the approach, the rider must give the greatest attention to following the movements of the horse's head and neck with semi-relaxed shoulders, elbows, and hands. The hands, at this critical period, must not distract the attention of the horse from the jump. *The elbows, particularly, must open and close with elastic smoothness, in follow-ing the mouth. Upon arriving at the point of take-off, the tension should never be heavier than the normal feel, and with a trustworthy horse, it is preferable to have the lightest contact possible.* Members of the Army Horse Show Team when jumping in competition, often held the reins between the thumbs and forefingers only, in order that the arms and hands could not involuntarily be contracted and so pull the horse. Holding the reins in the above fashion permits the horse to pull them entirely loose, unless the hands follow the movements of the mouth.

If the horse is properly in front of the rider's legs, the lighter the tension on the reins is, just prior to the take-off, the easier he can be controlled. This is true because the muscles of the neck and jaw are relaxed; there is no pull against the bit to resist. Therefore, the slightest effect with the fingers on the reins will cause the horse to flex momentarily and serve to decrease his speed, keep him straight on his course, or change direction. Keeping the horse straight toward the center of his obstacle during the approach, is very important. Approaching at an angle makes a run-out easy and tempts the horse to try it.

Plate XLV *Feet not home in stirrups; knees too high and too far to front; loin and back humped; rider "back of horse." Compare with Plates IX and XIV.*

Plate XLVI *Downward thrust of head and neck, aiding forelegs to clear obstacle.*

A horseman should always sit down in his saddle during the last fifteen or twenty yards of the approach. If standing in the stirrups, he is unable to feel what the horse is preparing to do, and as a result cannot prevent refusals or run-outs, and never knows at what exact stride the horse will take-off. Moreover, with the weight in the stirrups, his legs are not tightly closed against the horse's sides, which prevents their acting with sufficient promptness and vigor when occasion demands. As in all else, the legs play a prominent role in jumping.

When seated for the approach, the buttocks should be well to the rear, the loin hollowed-out, the heels driven far down, and the calves and knees glued to the saddle and horse. The body should retain the same marked forward inclination that it has when standing in the stirrups. The tendency to sit up a little straighter should be avoided, since, from the moment of take-off until landing is completed, the rider should be standing in the stirrups. (See Plate XXIV.)

The good horseman remains quietly in balance during the approach and take-off. Any sliding forward in the saddle, or unnecessary swaying forward and backward, disturbs the horse's equilibrium and distracts his attention at a time when all his faculties are concentrated on placing himself for his take-off.

Normally, at about fifteen yards from the obstacle, after the horse has been rated and the rider is seated in balance, the legs should administer a strong squeeze with the calves, or, in dealing with a timid or unreliable hunter or jumper, a hard pinch with the spurs. The purpose of this leg action is to push the horse momentarily onto his bit more firmly and establish more impulsion from the hind legs by engaging them under him. He is also thus notified that the decision to take the jump has been definitely made, and his only part is immediate execution. After this notification, the calves remain closely clamped to his sides, urging him steadily forward, and ready to act vigorously with the spurs in case he hesitates during the approach. Horses all differ in sensibility to the legs' action, so the rider's tact must regulate their vigor. However, if an error in the amount of vigor is made, be certain that it is on the vigorous side. With a horse prone to refuse, it is advisable to take no chances, but to give him a decisive blow with the spurs when he first sees the obstacle. He then still has time to settle down from its effect and measure his take-off. The legs continue to act moderately all the way to the jump.

Plate XLVII *Engagement of hocks. Neck and head beginning downward thrust. Note that rider is thrown out of saddle by raising of forehand; not by thrust of hind legs.*

Plate XLVIII *Forelegs having cleared, head and neck raise, forcing shoulders down and croup up. Bascule begins. Rider remains out of saddle. Reins two inches too long.*

Just for a second or two when the legs first act at the beginning of the approach, the hands should resist somewhat if the horse is not strongly on his bit. The instant he accepts it, they begin to follow his mouth. Certain horses depart for the obstacle with a rush. These do not need the leg action at the beginning of the approach. However, if at first they must be restrained, they should be given a lighter feel on the bit progressively, and not by a sudden abandonment of the reins. More important still, the legs must begin to act when nearing the obstacle. There is no horse which will not refuse, sooner or later, if the legs are passive, just prior to, and at, the take-off. Usually, there is more than normal tension on the reins, due to the necessity of rating most horses when the approach begins. In all these cases, the reins must be fed out progressively, until the normal feel is established. It is a mistake to allow the horse to rush at the jump from a great distance. He usually becomes sprawled-out, or refuses, after escaping the bit.

During the last few strides, there is always a moment when it appears that the horse has measured his strides badly and is "in wrong" for the take-off. *At this disturbing moment, the rider must resist the strong inclination to contract his fingers and elbows, while allowing the legs to "go limp."* This reaction to the instinct of self-preservation must be overcome. When the approach appears all wrong, more than ever must the rider relax sufficiently to sit still in the saddle, maintain his forward inclination, decontract the muscles of arms and hands, follow the horse's head, and increase the squeeze of the legs. In the next fraction of a second, if these directions have been followed, the situation will invariably clear up. The rider's passive hands having left the horse to his own devices, he, urged also by the same instinct of self-preservation, as well as the decisive action of the rider's legs, will place himself correctly and negotiate the jump with ease. The approach demands from the horseman, fast thinking and excellent coordination. He must maintain his balance, seat, and muscular control, without stiffening or standing in his stirrups.

It is noteworthy that most all mistakes at an obstacle are made as a result of the horse's getting too close when taking off. "Getting too close" is caused by the restraining influence of apprehensive hands, lack of deciding action by the legs, or lameness or soreness in the horse. Poor hands, which jerk a horse's mouth during the jump, soon make him afraid to jump boldly, since the bigger the jump, the harder the jerk. He creeps closer and closer at each successive jump, and if the punishment continues, ends by refusing.

Plate XLIX *Result of losing seat during approach. Heels up; knees slipped loose; back humped.*

Plate L *Beautiful form resulting from keeping seat during approach.*

The horse should be encouraged, during all his training, to take long, free jumps in his stride. Teaching him to jump in the stride does not mean that the rider should make the serious mistake of over-riding, by violently spurring, flopping his arms, and swaying the body back and forth during the approach. Such wild actions upset the horse and lead to falls. A good horseman endeavors to carry his horse along freely and boldly, with light hands and strong legs, instilling courage and confidence, but avoiding excitement. The legs are always active on any horse during the approach, gently encouraging him to "jump big."

Riding During Take-Off

At the take-off and during two or three strides prior to it, the squeeze of the legs should be particularly strong, and the spurs, ready to pinch the horse at any indication of a refusal. The contact with the mouth should have become progressively lighter during the approach, and at the moment of the take-off, should be exceedingly gentle. As the forelegs leave the ground, — never before, — it is best to allow all contact to vanish, except that maintained by the weight of the reins. The reins may have even a slight sag in them immediately after the forelegs leave the ground, all during the period of suspension, and when landing. It is astounding to see the difficult situations from which a horse can extricate himself during a jump, *if the rider's reins are slack*. Unless the hands are excellent, let the reins go slack after the take-off.

Many of the best hunters and jumpers start their approach for an obstacle with a rush. Upon nearing it, they check their speed suddenly, bunch themselves, and shorten the last two or three strides before taking off. With such horses, the rider must be well forward, when the rush starts to avoid falling back out of balance, which will cause pulling on the reins. Also the sudden checking and abrupt shortening of the stride, commonly referred to as "propping," make it difficult for the rider to maintain his position and balance. His seat tends to slide forward in the saddle, and his lower legs slip to the rear in a helpless position. This not only deprives him of the power to use his legs, and of his security of seat, but also disturbs the horse's equilibrium and calculations for the take-off. Moreover, due to losing his position in the saddle, contact with the horse's mouth is suddenly abandoned. The interference with his equilibrium, and the sudden loss of support from the rider's hands, often cause the horse to refuse. *It is only by keeping the heels driven far down, the legs and knees tightly against horse and saddle, and the buttocks pushed well to the rear by keeping the loin concave, that the rider can prevent any dislocation of his seat.* If the seat is not deranged, he will not lose contact with the horse's mouth, nor the use of his legs. Accord

Plate LI *Beautiful balance. Rider's hands correctly following horse's mouth.*

between himself and the horse will exist, and there will be no refusal. *He will have a sensation of pushing his seat to the rear as the horse checks, while at the same time he can drive the horse forward with his legs.* Keeping the heels down, which allows the feet to brace against the stirrups, while the legs urge the horse on, is the only way that this can be accomplished.

Refusals

With a refusing horse, contact with the mouth must be maintained until he actually leaves the ground with his fore feet at the take-off. In order to stop at a jump, if he is going along at a good pace, he must lower his head. To duck his head, he first must escape contact with the hand. *Therefore, with a refuser, contact must never be lost.* At the same time, the rider's legs must act more vigorously than usual, since the feel on the mouth must be heavier to prevent escaping the bit and ducking the head. *It is, however, very necessary that the hands follow the mouth while maintaining the heavier contact.* The usual error is committed through fixing the hands or pulling, when keeping the horse's head up, which by immobilizing his head and neck, prevents his placing himself, and makes it physically impossible for him to jump. Almost invariably, a refuser ducks his head either to the right or left when stopping. After determining which side he habitually chooses, the opposite rein should have a little greater tension during the last few strides. As usual, after being forced to jump, he should be given his head entirely as he takes off.

Oftentimes a rider will arrive at the take-off with a heavier tension on the reins than he usually maintains. This may be the result of apprehension, miscalculation, or the fact that his horse has bolted too fast at the jump. In any case, the fatal error of suddenly abandoning the reins one, two, or three strides in front of the obstacle, must never be made. It may cause a grave accident, since the horse is completely unbalanced by this sudden loss of strong support.

Riding During Period of Suspension

Motion pictures prove that the rider's seat leaves the saddle at the take-off, as a result of the horse's checking and lifting his forehand; not as a result of the extension and propulsion of the hind legs, as is generally believed. (See Plate XLVII). Consequently a forward seat favors the shoulders in their work of lifting the rider's mass at the take-off. He should, from the moment he is thrust forward and upward, remain out of the saddle during the entire period of suspension, as well as while landing. This is accomplished by partly stiffening the knee joints and remaining balanced over the knees, stirrups, and heels. He is actually standing in the stirrups (See Chapter II), with almost all his weight settled in the heels of his boots. If the ankle joints are relaxed, the weight, perforce, drives the heels well down and forces the calves against the horse. The calves and knees by their grip aid greatly in maintaining the position and balance. The angle at the hip closes, and that at the knee opens, as a result of the upward thrust out of the saddle. The back muscles must be immediately tightened, and remain so, while passing over the jump, in order to keep the loin hollowed out and give muscular control of the trunk. This control of the trunk, in a large measure, is what permits the rider to stay in balance.

The important points for the rider to remember during the period of suspension are: first; the horse makes the gesture of extending his neck and lowering his head, to help his forehand over the jump. The hands must therefore feed out all the rein necessary, by extending the arms, and in no case, interfere with the gesture by jerking his mouth. Secondly; the instant the forehand has cleared, the head and neck are thrown upward, forcing the forelegs down, and helping to lift the hindquarters over the obstacle. The rider should stay out of the saddle and well forward. Sitting down at this instant will interfere greatly with the hind legs' clearing. On the other hand, remaining forward helps tip the descending forehand downward, and aids the horse's efforts. (See Plate LI.)

Riding During Landing

This phase begins the instant the hind legs have cleared the obstacle. The horse's forehand is descending. The rider's arms are well extended, to give sufficient rein; his back remains straight and hollowed out, and the brace against the stirrups again is necessary to prevent sliding forward in the saddle as the horse lands. The trunk has been inclined far forward from the hips as the horse rose and cleared the obstacle. As he starts downward, the rider's closed hip joints begin to open and the knee joints to close; he slightly straightens his trunk to move his center of gravity backward and maintain his balance over his knees, as the momentum of the jump dies out. As the descent begins, the horse pivots about his own center of gravity and between the rider's knees, bringing the saddle close to the crotch and buttocks. The rider should not, however, sit down, but remain balanced, in the stirrups, with the help of the knees. During the entire period, the reins should exert no tension whatever. They cannot assist the horse while he is in the air, whereas their mildest action on the bit may greatly militate against his efforts. The fingers should always remain relaxed and half open, during the entire jump.

As the fore feet land, there is, as has been described, another up and down gesture of head and neck in assisting the front feet to hop out of the way of the descending hind feet. During this time, unless it is necessary to

Plate LII *Fraction of second before landing. Note brace on stirrups and fixing of back muscles. Fingers relaxed.*

Plate LIII *One foreleg grounded. Note great strain on horse. Rider tense, to remain out of saddle. All weight in stirrups and on knees. Martingale is a trifle too short.*

Plate LIV *Rider's legs slipped to rear. All weight on knees. Seat unstable.*

Plate LV *Lower legs in correct position. Form perfect.*

immediately change direction, the reins remain lightly stretched or slack. The rider should gently collect them and establish the normal feel as the horse takes his first strides, in resuming the gallop. In the meantime, the rider continues to remain out of the saddle, which prevents thumping the horse's back as he lands. The ankles, knees, and hip joints may close slightly to soften the jar at this time. The body should not be allowed to flop far forward. This can be avoided by using the back's muscles to keep the back straight and the loin hollowed out. After the gallop is resumed and the reins are collected, the rider gently sits down in the saddle, if approaching another obstacle. Thoughtless riders are inclined to sit down heavily as the horse lands, and snatch the reins taut. The horse interprets the painful effects as punishment associated with jumping, and soon begins to rush, refuse, or bolt. Landing is an ungraceful and difficult phase for horse and rider. The brace on the stirrups, pinch with the knees, and force exerted by the back muscles, to maintain balance, are extreme, after the horse jumps "big." (See Plates LII and LIII.) The strain on the horse's forelegs is very great.

Throughout the jump, and especially at landing, the knees pinch the saddle strongly and remain fixed in place. The lower legs, (calves), squeeze the horse until the take-off is actually made, whereupon the rider's weight goes into the stirrups. He voluntarily keeps it in them throughout the jump, and while the lower legs feel close to the horse, they move somewhat, since the stirrup-straps remain approximately vertical during all phases, due to the weight in the stirrups. It is a common and bad fault to allow the lower legs to swing to the rear, through riding entirely on the knees and not in the stirrups, during the jump. It weakens the seat and leaves the rider very unstable. (Compare Plates LIV. and LV.)

Resume

These remarks on jumping may be epitomized as follows:

The approach; — body inclined forward from hips, quietly in balance; hands follow mouth; legs active up to and including take-off; leg pressure increases gradually, rein tension decreases; horse directed perpendicularly toward center of obstacle.

The take-off; — trunk and seat still; legs active; hands passive; rein tension very light.

The period of suspension; — rider out of saddle continuously, in balance in stirrups; back muscles, knees, and hips function in maintaining balance; very light or no tension on reins.

The landing; — rider remains standing in stirrups; very light or no tension on reins; normal contact resumed after landing is completed.

XENOPHON PRESS LIBRARY
www.XenophonPress.com

Xenophon Press is dedicated to the preservation of classical equestrian literature. We bring both new and old works to English-speaking riders.

30 Years with Master Nuno Oliveira, Henriquet 2011

A New Method to Dress Horses, Cavendish 2020

A Rider's Survival from Tyranny, de Kunffy 2012

Another Horsemanship, Racinet 1994

Austrian Art of Riding, Poscharnigg 2015

Classic Show Jumping: the de Nemethy Method, de Nemethy 2016

Divide and Conquer Book 1, Lemaire de Ruffieu 2016

Divide and Conquer Book 2, Lemaire de Ruffieu 2017

Dressage for the 21st Century, Belasik 2001

Dressage in the French Tradition, Diogo de Bragança 2011

Dressage Principles and Techniques: A Blueprint for the Serious Rider, Tavora 2018

Dressage Principles Illuminated, Expanded Edition, de Kunffy 2020

Dressage Sabbatical: A Year of Riding with Classical Master Paul Belasik, Caslar 2016

École de Cavalerie Part II, Robichon de la Guérinière 1992, 2015

Equine Osteopathy: What the Horses Have Told Me, Giniaux 2014

Fragments from the Writings of Max Ritter von Weyrother, Fane 2017

François Baucher: The Man and His Method, Baucher/Nelson 2013

General Chamberlin: America's Equestrian Genius, Matha 2020

Great Horsewomen of the 19th Century in the Circus, Nelson 2015

Gymnastic Exercises for Horses Volume II, Eleanor Russell 2013

H. Dv. 12 German Cavalry Manual of Horsemanship, Reinhold 2014

Handbook of Jumping Essentials, Lemaire de Ruffieu 2015

Handbook of Riding Essentials, Lemaire de Ruffieu 2015

Healing Hands, Giniaux, DVM 1998

Horse Training: Outdoors and High School, Beudant 2014

I, Siglavy, Asay 2018

Learning to Ride, Santini 2016

Legacy of Master Nuno Oliveira, Millham 2013

Lessons in Lightness: The Art of Educating the Horse, Mark Russell 2016

Lessons in Lightness: Expanded Edition, Mark Russell 2019

Methodical Dressage of the Riding Horse, Faverot de Kerbrech 2010

Military Equitation: or, A Method of Breaking Horses, and Teaching Soldiers to Ride, Pembroke, *and A Treatise on Military Equitation,* Tyndale 2018

Principles of Dressage and Equitation, a.k.a. Breaking and Riding, Fillis 2017

Racinet Explains Baucher, Racinet 1997

Riding and Schooling Horses, Chamberlin 2020

Riding by Torchlight, Cord 2019

Science and Art of Riding in Lightness, Stodulka 2015

The Art of Riding a Horse, D'Eisenberg 2015

The Art of Traditional Dressage, Volume I DVD, de Kunffy 2013

The de Nemethy Method: A training seminar, 8 DVD set, de Nemethy 2019

The Ethics and Passions of Dressage Expanded Edition, de Kunffy 2013

The Forward Impulse, Santini 2016

The Gymnasium of the Horse, Steinbrecht 2018

The Horses, a novel, Elaine Walker 2015

The Italian Tradition of Equestrian Art, Tomassini 2014

The Maneige Royal, de Pluvinel 2010, 2015

The Portuguese School of Equestrian Art, de Oliveira/da Costa 2012

The Spanish Riding School & Piaffe and Passage, Decarpentry 2013

To Amaze the People with Pleasure and Delight, Walker 2015

Total Horsemanship, Racinet 1999

Training Hunters, Jumpers, and Hacks, Chamberlin 2019

Training with Master Nuno Oliveira, 2 DVD set, Eleanor Russell 2016

Truth in the Teaching of Master Nuno Oliveira, Eleanor Russell 2015

Wisdom of Master Nuno Oliveira, de Coux 2012

www.ingramcontent.com/pod-product-compliance
Lightning Source LLC
Chambersburg PA
CBHW082104280426
43661CB00089B/857